SHAKESPEARE'S COMEDIES

SHAKESPEARE'S COMEDIES

BARNES & NOBLE FOCUS BOOKS

PLOT OUTLINES OF
Shakespeare's Comedies
SCENE BY SCENE

J. WILSON McCUTCHAN, PH.D.

Professor of English
University of Waterloo

BARNES & NOBLE, INC.

PUBLISHERS · BOOKSELLERS · SINCE 1873

This is an original Focus Book (Number 710). It was written by a distinguished educator, carefully edited, and produced in accordance with the highest standards of publishing. The text was set on the Linotype in Old Style, Caledonia, and Electra by Hamilton Printing Company (Rensselaer, N.Y.). The paper for this edition was manufactured by S. D. Warren Company (Boston, Mass.) and supplied by Canfield Paper Company (New York, N. Y.). This edition was printed by Hamilton Printing Company and bound by Sendor Bindery (New York, N.Y.). The cover was designed by Rod Lopez-Fabrega.

TABLE OF CONTENTS

READING SHAKESPEARE'S PLAYS [1]

"A play read, affects the mind like a play acted."
Samuel Johnson
Preface to Shakespeare (1765)

Drama is one of the oldest forms of literary entertainment. Almost every person, young or old, enjoys going to a theater, watching a motion picture, or viewing a good show on television. One explanation for drama's popularity is that a play appeals to the physical senses of sight and hearing simultaneously. This dual perception also enables a playwright to compress much material within relatively short space and time.

Closet Drama versus Stage Drama

Sometimes an author writes "closet drama"—a form intended for reading rather than acting—but writers usually expect actors and actresses to present their plays before an audience. Shakespeare and his contemporaries wrote for the stage.

Effective play production requires extensive preparation from many different people. Also, a theater with an adequate stage and ample seating facilities must be available. These factors make professional play production expensive. Consequently, this cultural asset is regularly a feature of large cities or of places that support or subsidize seasonal theaters. Little theaters, university, college, and high school dramatic organizations, and other amateur groups often give pleasing performances, but these attractions usually run for short periods only. In the United States, the number of people who can see plays in a playhouse is a small part of the total population.

Many people, therefore, must substitute the reading of plays for witnessing them on a stage. Although a live production is the preferable way of enjoying a play, intelligent and imaginative reading can afford many advantages and pleasures. Some of these may equal

---

[1] Based in part upon "Suggestions on Reading Shakespeare," in Homer A. Watt, Karl J. Holzknecht, and Raymond Ross, *Outlines of Shakespeare's Plays* (New York: Barnes & Noble, Inc., 1957).

those of actually attending the play; in fact, many devotees of the live stage like to read a play both before and after seeing a performance.

These benefits of reading plays are especially evident when a person examines older works like those of Shakespeare and his fellow Elizabethans. Shakespeare was a poet as well as a playwright. His plays tell stories that have interested readers and audiences for centuries; they also give pictures of life and of human beings facing life's problems. Because he wrote some four hundred years ago, his plays contain many allusions, words, and idioms unfamiliar today. Most misleading of these are words that have remained in use but have changed in meaning. Careful reading may thus reveal ideas which a person easily overlooks or misses when he is watching the same play in a theater.

The Actor's Contribution

True, competent actors often give Shakespeare's poetic lines a conversational quality that "brings them to life." By means of intonations, pauses, facial expressions, and gestures they can impart added significance to many passages. At the same time, actors and directors frequently interpret action and characters according to their own ideas, and sometimes an audience leaves a theater without realizing that other interpretations are equally possible and valid.

For example, when Mark Antony delivers his speech over Caesar's body, he repeatedly describes Brutus and the other conspirators with the word *honourable*. Much of an audience's understanding of this address and of Antony himself depends on the tone and stress with which the actor playing Antony pronounces this word. In the beginning, Antony seems to use *honourable* as a plain description of character; at the end of his oration the word has become bitingly sarcastic. With this one word a skillful actor can color a viewer's concept of the role. In *Othello,* when Iago is poisoning Othello's mind against Desdemona, he rouses his master to frenzy through his enunciation of simple and "innocent" words such as *indeed* and *honest* (III,iii, 101,103). When Macbeth wavers in his resolution to kill Duncan, Lady Macbeth reassures him by exclaiming, "We fail!" An actress's rendering of these two words may give an audience great insight into Lady Macbeth's personality and determination. By his own reading and rereading of speeches and lines like these, a person can enrich his appreciation of Shakespeare's close observation of life and of his skill as a playwright. Furthermore, as the reader becomes aware of the diversity and shadings of interpretation, he realizes that many of Shakespeare's characters resemble real men and women in a way which defies specific classification and analysis.

The Reader's Advantage

Another advantage for the reader is that he may study a play in the form in which editors believe Shakespeare wrote it. Modern directors, for various reasons, frequently find it desirable or necessary to shorten the text, rearrange the sequence of scenes, or eliminate certain characters. Every production is likely to vary somewhat from other productions of the same play. Different actors portray the same role in different ways. Veteran actors may change lines or unintentionally alter the presentation of a character from one performance to the next. Because a careful reader can envision scenes and imagine characters according to his own judgment and taste, he enjoys a freedom and independence which he does not always retain as a member of an actual audience in a theater.

Reading Aloud

One of the most profitable ways in which to learn Shakespeare's plays is to read them aloud. Small groups of people have increased their understanding and knowledge of these works by assigning themselves parts and reading the lines as if they were taking roles in a stage production. A lone reader can also derive definite benefits from reading aloud and permitting his ears to assist his eyes in comprehending the speeches. If a reader pronounces words as naturally as possible, the dialogue becomes more like the conversation of real people and sounds less like a quotation from a literary classic.

Also, reading aloud tends to dispel the mysterious quality that poetry has for many persons. A conscientious reader will find that good poetry becomes an asset rather than an obstacle. Shakepeare's blank verse will impart a rhythm which helps the reader to remember lines after he has finished the play. At times, the sheer beauty of a lyrical passage is inescapable, as in Mercutio's description of Queen Mab in *Romeo and Juliet*. Experienced actors testify that they find it easier to memorize Shakespeare's lines than they do dialogue from modern prose plays. Any careful reader may exploit and enjoy this poetic asset.

Whether a person reads aloud or silently, he should not hurry. He should regard his reading as an opportunity to meet a vast number of men and women in all kinds of situations rather than view it as another chore. The reader should always remember that Shakespeare was more interested in entertaining than in teaching and that he expected people to find amusement and cause for reflection in his plays rather than to take tests and examinations on them.

The Reader's Imagination

Shakespeare relied heavily on the imagination of his audience. He did not attempt to provide a complete physical representation of every detail of his drama. If the rehearsal scenes of the craftsmen in *A Midsummer Night's Dream*, for example, he good-naturedly parodies the amateur actors who insist that moonshine, wall, and lion must assume physical stage personalities. Shakespeare expected that men and women filling the Globe Theatre would listen as well as watch and that they would permit their own fancy to round out the characters and situations which his poetry suggested. He understood that each person's mind could supply details exceeding those within the descriptive power of any playwright. Although he liked to remind his audience of the similarities between situations on the stage and life outside the playhouse ("All the world's a stage,/And all the men and women merely players," Jaques observes in *As You Like It*), he always remembered the illusory and make-believe quality of the theater. After the masque in *The Tempest*, Prospero says,

> Our revels now are ended. These our actors,
> As I foretold you, were all spirits and
> Are melted into air, into thin air;
> And, like the baseless fabric of this vision,
> The cloud-capp'd towers, the gorgeous palaces,
> The solemn temples, the great globe itself,
> Yea, all which it inherit, shall dissolve,
> And, like this insubstantial pageant faded,
> Leave not a rack behind. (IV,i)

Few theaters can provide realistic enactments of battle scenes when fifteen or twenty actors on each side are as many as most stages can accommodate. No make-up artist can transform an actor or actress into a completely convincing Oberon, Titania, Ariel, Caliban, Ghost of Hamlet's father, or Witch in *Macbeth*. What may be a satisfactory representation to one viewer often strikes another as fantastic or comic. In the "mind's eye," however, each reader can supply those features which to him are most ethereal, supernatural, gruesome, awesome. Here again he may permit his imagination to carry him into realms of reality surpassing those which any producer or director can project on stage or screen.

Readers have similar opportunities to produce the setting and atmosphere, the physical characters, and the action in their "mental theaters." Dialogue thus becomes more than a succession of statements and responses; it is the lively interchange of thought, passion, ambition, love, hate, suspicion. Shakespeare was an economical writer; he did not waste words on creative effort. Descriptive passages are as essential to the understanding of a play as are vigorous lines and violent action. When the gentle and unsuspecting Duncan approaches Inverness, he remarks,

> This castle hath a pleasant seat. The air
> Nimbly and sweetly recommends itself
> Unto our gentle senses. (*Macbeth*, I,vi, 1–3)

In his imagination the reader can envision the arrival of the royal party more vividly and completely than any designer or stage manager can represent it; he may also shudder at the grim irony of the innocent Duncan's seeking the restful hospitality of the castle which is to be the scene of his murder. In this way a drama becomes more than a faint and far-off series of incidents, and its people emerge as more than bloodless and impersonal figures or the costumed and painted forms of favorite stage personalities. No one should view a Shakespearian play as merely an exercise in sixteenth-century vocabulary or as an introduction to Elizabethan grammar.

The Reader as Confidant

Partly because of the physical demands and limitations of his playhouses, and partly because of his own genius, Shakespeare did more than most dramatists to enable readers to make their own dramatic reconstructions. From one point of view, his plays prove quite easy to read. He takes his audience and readers so completely into his confidence that it often seems as if they are helping him to plot the action. Some characters deceive, puzzle, and hoodwink other characters; they almost never surprise or deceive the audience or reader. Julia, Portia and Nerissa, Rosalind, and Viola disguise themselves as young men and trick their lovers; the reader knows who they are and enjoys their masquerading. In *Hamlet* and *Macbeth*, the audience knows who has committed crimes, who is plot-

ting others, and why. Aaron, Richard III, Iago, and Edmund dupe
their respective victims, but before he acts each has painstakingly
revealed his intended villainy to the reader. When Hamlet berates
his mother in her apartment, she and Polonius believe that the prince
is at the point of harming her physically, but Hamlet has previously
advised the audience that he "will speak daggers to her, but use
none."

The Reader as Participant

In the practical jokes of the comedies the reader becomes a par-
ticipant along with the pranksters themselves. He overhears Maria
and Sir Toby Belch plotting the humiliation of Malvolio; he listens
to the merry wives of Windsor as they plan to mock the fat Falstaff.

In tragedy, the reader finds evil more terrible because he watches
it slowly entangling unfortunate men and women in its web. In
comedy, he gets greater enjoyment in observing the blind folly of
stupid people because he shares in exposing it.

Rereading

Every Shakespearian play calls for more than one reading. The
first reading for the story should be fairly rapid. Subsequent read-
ings, slower and more methodical, reveal plot structure, subtleties
of characterization, word clusters, imagery, and other elements that
grow in significance as the reader's familiarity with the text increases.
Anyone will find it helpful to make notes on a pad or in the margins
and to underline passages that strike him as meaningful or important.
Each reading exposes facets of Shakespeare's skill that the reader
has overlooked before and that increase his understanding of the
drama. A few suggestions for this kind of study follow.

Classifying the Play

First, the reader should determine the type of play he has at
hand. Most complete editions group Shakespeare's plays under three
headings: comedies, histories, tragedies. Shakespeare, however, frequently mixed his forms, and such a division does not always cover
one particular play. *Richard II* and *1 Henry IV* are both history
plays, but the first is tragic whereas the second is essentially comic.
As You Like It and *Twelfth Night* are romantic comedies; the first
is also a pastoral comedy, but the second is not. *The Comedy of
Errors* blends farce with romantic comedy; *The Merry Wives of
Windsor* is largely farce; *Love's Labour's Lost* is a court comedy.

Troilus and Cressida has proved especially troublesome to critics determined to classify it.

Although the reader may wish to identify the play he is reading, he should not feel compelled to place it in one of the three traditional categories. Whatever else it may be, it remains *a play*.

Setting of the Play

Shakespeare approached much of his material from a romanticist's point of view, and many of his plays depict events in a romantic and vague past and in foreign countries such as Greece, Italy, France, or the New World. At the same time, these plays contain much that is realistic. His princes are Venetian, Ephesian, or Athenian in name, but they are English in personality and character; his mobs are English as well as Roman. Often he ignores the historical date of the action and introduces contemporary settings, episodes, and people, as he does in the Boar's Head Tavern scenes in *1* and *2 Henry IV*. Noting these various elements will broaden the reader's appreciation of the play's plot, characters, locale, and themes.

The Play's Sources

Because Shakespeare borrowed his stories from chronicles, prose fiction, old plays, and narrative poems, and seldom bothered to invent his own plots, a person might suppose that he followed such sources faithfully. He did not. He added, omitted, and changed incidents and characters to fit his ideas of what made a good play. As a result, he often fashioned exciting drama from shopworn and rather dull materials. A comparison of one of Shakespeare's plays with its sources is interesting because it may throw light on his skill and on his notion of what constituted effective drama, but such a comparison is not necessary for an appreciation of the play itself.

Tragedy and Comedy

Drama has its basis in human conflict. In tragedy, this conflict ends in disaster; in comedy it results in happiness or reconciliation. In tragedy, this struggle springs from passions that possess the hearts and minds of men and women—ambition, hatred, greed, lust, and other emotions that poison the souls of their victims. In comedy, the conflict usually derives from rivalry in love, from the effort of a banished ruler to regain his throne, or from the recovery of family or fortune.

A reader will not find it easy or even possible to reduce Shakespeare's works to a single formula, but most of his plays present to a knowing audience and discerning reader the spectacle of mankind groping its way through life, to catastrophe in tragedy or to success and satisfaction in comedy. Tragedy ends with death, comedy usually with one or more marriages. A funeral dirge accompanies one, just as wedding nights do the other.

Plotting of the Play

Synopses and summaries are incapable of revealing Shakespeare's artistry in employing sub-plots, side-plots, and parallel plots so as to increase the audience's understanding of the main plot and major characters. He interwove these ingredients so skillfully that the effect is that of one play, not of two or more artificially tied together. An illustration will clarify this structural technique: In the main plot of *King Lear*, Lear disinherits the loving and loyal Cordelia and bestows his kingdom on her two cruel and hypocritical sisters, who proceed to abuse their old father. Guilty of mental and spiritual excesses, Lear suffers unbearable emotional torment. In the minor plot, Edmund, bastard son of the Earl of Gloucester, tricks his father into disowning Edgar, the faithful and legitimate son. Gloucester's most obvious weakness has been indulgence of his physical passions, and he endures horrible physical agony when his enemies gouge out his eyes. Goneril's and Regan's persecution of Gloucester, their lust for the illegitimate Edmund, the knavery of Oswald, the execution of Cordelia, and other devices combine the two plots. The reader should always examine such mechanics of dramatic construction carefully and consider the relationship of all the parts to one another.

Shakespeare's plots depend on his people. Action results from the moods, emotions, and activities of main characters. A dramatic consistency exists between persons and incidents; things happen because people act and interact on each other. If a reader imagines that a character in one play might take a role in another, then he can see how sure and meticulous Shakespeare was in depicting human beings in certain situations. What might Rosalind or Beatrice have done in Perdita's place, or in Miranda's? Think of Hamlet married to Desdemona and subject to Iago's malevolence! Such mental gymnastics can produce no definite conclusions, but they enable a reader to appreciate Shakespeare's capacity for assigning accurate and specific actions to characters under the stress of particular problems. A thorough acquaintance with the principal characters is, therefore, essential for an understanding of a play as a whole.

Characterization

Students can analyze dramatic characters in much the same fashion as they come to know human beings in real life. People learn to evaluate others in numerous ways: by what they say and how they say it, and oftentimes by their silence or refusal to say anything at all. People's behavior under stress or their failure to act in certain crises often reveals much about them. Others who know them or have had dealings with them frequently describe them aptly and accurately. Some of Shakespeare's characters are frank and rough in their speech, make off-color puns, and enjoy salacious jokes. In such portrayals of human nature, Shakespeare was merely realistic and practical. His grooms, whores, innkeepers, soldiers, and rascals use the language of their station and trade. His schoolteachers talk like teachers, his kings and queens like monarchs, his grooms and nursemaids like domestic servants. His men and women consistently communicate in the vocabulary and idiom of their social class and at the same time disclose their individual nature and mannerisms. Each person's speech tells the reader much about his personality.

Similarly, a character's confidential conversations with other characters may reveal as much as do his soliloquies and asides. Hamlet's private chats with Horatio and Portia's intimate talks with Nerissa add to the audience's understanding of the melancholy prince and of the beautiful heiress, just as Hotspur's dialogue with his wife bares a more human and softer side of the fire-eating rebel.

Frequently a reader gains additional insight into the nature of a major character through comments about him. Julius Caesar gives a vivid and accurate description of Cassius:

> Yond Cassius has a lean and hungry look.
> He thinks too much. Such men are dangerous.
> . . . .
> Such men as he be never at heart's ease
> Whiles they behold a greater than themselves,
> And therefore are they very dangerous.
>
> (*Julius Caesar*, I,ii, 194–195, 208–210)

In *The Merchant of Venice* Portia assesses her suitors in frank and critical fashion, and in *Antony and Cleopatra* Enobarbus supplies shrewd and penetrating explanations of the Egyptian queen's spell over the Roman general.

Character Foils

Quite often a person's nature and personality stand out most clearly when they contrast with those of another individual. The technical term for a role that provides such a contrast is *character foil*. Shakespeare was fond of using these contrasting opposites, or *foils*. Falstaff is fat, Shallow thin; Hermia is a small brunette, Helena a statuesque blonde. More frequently the differences lie in temperament. In *The Comedy of Errors*, Adriana is sharp-tongued and shrewish; her sister Luciana is sweet, placid, tolerant. In *1 Henry IV*, Hotspur will drop everything to seek glory and bloodshed on the battlefield; Prince Hal prefers the roistering, carefree companionship of Falstaff and his cronies. Macbeth's impatient ambition and ruthlessness appear more inhuman than they really are when the reader contrasts them with Banquo's fidelity and patience.

Setting

In corresponding fashion, each reader can envision the background and setting of every play. Shakespeare usually supplied the barest descriptions of scenes and the scantiest stage directions. Clues for these come largely from dialogue. As a reader assembles and lists these features, he can readily see the care with which Shakespeare conceived and blended all the ingredients of his dramas. The desolate heath in *Macbeth*, the storm raging over King Lear and his small band on the moor, the idyllic Forest of Arden in *As You Like It*, Olivia's typically Tudor household in *Twelfth Night*—these and many other scenes attest Shakespeare's attention to the balancing of setting, characters, and action.

Shakespeare's Universality

Still another advantage of reading and rereading these plays is that a person becomes increasingly aware of Shakespeare's universality as a writer. By imagining *Julius Caesar* in a modern setting, the reader can see that, although the play dramatizes a bloody episode in Roman history, it also presents a graphic picture of honest men and unscrupulous men striving for power in a military state and maneuvering for political influence. A similar play today might depict tycoons trying to gain control of some large industry or financial empire. Whether or not such struggles involve assassinations and riots, the ethics, temptations, and personal decisions confronting individuals are basically the same as those facing Brutus, Cassius, and Antony. Brutus, confident of his own integrity and public spirit, persuades himself that the necessity of protecting Rome from Caesar justifies an illegal and violent action. The specific question before Brutus is important and potentially tragic; the broad principle is one that every human being meets many times throughout life, whether he wears a business suit or a toga.

In comedy also, the thoughtful reader finds situations resembling those he has shared or observed. How often do a father and a daughter disagree over a suitor just as Egeus and Hermia do in *A Midsummer Night's Dream,* or as Silvia and the Duke of Milan do in *The Two Gentlemen of Verona*? Shylock's greatest fault lies not in his race or in his role as an avaricious and greedy moneylender, but in his refusal to show the quality of mercy when he has an opportunity to be merciful. Everyone, regardless of his business, profession, race, or age, faces similar opportunities again and again. When Rosalind, who has disguised herself as a young man, hears that Orlando is nearby, her immediate thought is to change her "slacks" for feminine attire. Henry V's efforts to overcome language barriers in his wooing of Katherine of France have countless parallels in the experiences of military men who have served their nations on foreign soil.

Summary

Every reader can become his own actor, his own director, and his own audience. The simple question, "How would I cast the play?" will focus attention on many details essential to knowing what Shakespeare probably intended. When Rosalind and Celia plan to escape into the forest, Rosalind says that it would be better that she wear man's clothing because she is "more than common tall." Anyone casting *As You Like It* must be certain that the actress playing Rosalind is taller than the one taking the part of her cousin. Also, the text indicates that Orlando has reddish hair.

Can *Othello* be effective with a white-skinned actor in the title role? Is Lady Macbeth tall and regal in appearance or short and vivacious? To these and many similar questions the reader has the privilege of giving his own answers, because professional and amateur producers must often make concessions to the personnel of their companies, to the availability of star performers, and to the conventions and attitudes of local audiences.

Finally, no one has to be an expert or a scholar to read Shakespeare's plays intelligently and profitably. In a remarkable way, every successive reading increases a thoughtful person's appreciation and understanding of a play. Practice indeed leads to perfection. Examination of what characters think and say, of how they look, of where they are, of what they do, enables the reader to know more about life and its problems and to become more confident in facing them.

SYNOPSES OF SHAKESPEARE'S COMEDIES

When studying, watching, or reviewing any play, a reader often wishes to recall the main events and sequence of the action or to locate characters quickly. As he increases his knowledge of Shakespeare's works, he frequently needs to refresh his memory on the plots, incidents, and characters of plays. This volume provides a ready and convenient reference for these purposes to the seventeen plays that most editors classify as comedies.

Users of this book should remember, however, that a synopsis is the barest outline of the basic elements of any drama and that it can never take the place of a thorough and conscientious reading and examination of the complete text. Helpful as a summary may be, it cannot convey the power, the subtlety, the magic of Shakespeare's genius as a master playwright and poet. Its best use therefore is to aid in reading or viewing the play.

THE COMEDY OF ERRORS [1592–1593]

CHARACTERS

SOLINUS, Duke of Ephesus.

AEGEON, a merchant of Syracuse.

ANTIPHOLUS of Ephesus, ANTIPHOLUS of Syracuse, } twin brothers, and sons to *Aegeon* and *Aemilia*.

DROMIO of Ephesus, DROMIO of Syracuse, } twin brothers, and attendants on the two *Antipholuses*.

BALTHAZAR, a merchant.

ANGELO, a goldsmith.

First Merchant, friend to *Antipholus* of Syracuse.

Second Merchant, to whom *Angelo* is a debtor.

PINCH, a schoolmaster.

AEMILIA, wife to *Aegeon*, an abbess at Ephesus.

ADRIANA, wife to *Antipholus* of Ephesus.

LUCIANA, her sister.

LUCE (also called NELL), servant to *Adriana*.

A Courtesan.

Jailor, Officers, and Attendants.

Scene: *Ephesus*

I,i. A Hall in the Palace of Solinus

Solinus, Duke of Ephesus, is explaining the laws of his city to Aegeon, a Syracusan under arrest and in the custody of the jailor. Because of past misunderstanding and disorder, the governments of Syracuse and Ephesus have forbidden commerce between their two cities. Any citizen of one town who is found in the other stands under penalty of death unless he can pay a fine of one thousand marks. Inasmuch as Aegeon has no money, he remarks that death will effectively release him from his woes. His curiosity aroused by Aegeon's statement, Solinus commands him to explain why he left Syracuse and came to Ephesus.

Aegeon recalls how in times of prosperity his wife accompanied

3

him on one of his business trips and gave birth to identical twin
sons (the Antipholuses). At the same hour and "in the self-same
inn" a poor woman likewise bore twin boys (the Dromios), whom
Aegeon purchased from their parents to serve as attendants to his
own sons. Then Aegeon and his household sailed for home.

In a violent storm the crew abandoned ship, leaving Aegeon and
his dependents aboard. Lashing themselves and the children to masts,
the travelers managed to survive the night only to crash on a rock
the next morning. Two ships sailed to their rescue and saved their
lives, but they separated Aegeon and the two infants with him from
Aemilia and the other Antipholus and Dromio.

At the age of eighteen Antipholus of Syracuse, with his father's
consent, took Dromio as his companion and left home to search for
his long-lost brother. Subsequently Aegeon devoted five years to
looking for his family through Greece and Asia. Unwilling to neglect
any city, he at last came to Ephesus.

Impressed with Aegeon's griefs and sympathetic to them, Solinus
grants the old man a day's time in which to look for friends and beg
or borrow the thousand marks necessary to redeem his life.

I,ii. The Mart [Market]

In transacting business with Antipholus of Syracuse, the First
Merchant, who has heard of Aegeon's arrest and sentence, advises
Antipholus to declare himself a native of Epidamnum lest he meet
with a similar fate. Antipholus gives a sum of money to his servant,
Dromio of Syracuse, with directions to keep it for him at the Cen-
taur Inn. Antipholus and the Merchant agree to meet that afternoon.

Walking alone to view the city, Antipholus meets Dromio of
Ephesus, whom he assumes to be his Dromio. In like fashion, Dromio
of Ephesus thinks that he is talking to his own master and calls him
to dinner. Surprised to see his servant so soon, Antipholus questions
him about the thousand marks he has recently entrusted to him.
Dromio naturally denies all knowledge of the money. In rising confusion, Antipholus beats Dromio, who scampers away. Fearing that
unprincipled Ephesians have bewitched or corrupted his servant, and
much concerned about his money, Antipholus starts for the Centaur
to investigate.

II,i. The House of Antipholus of Ephesus

Adriana, the wife of Antipholus of Ephesus, complains to her sister
Luciana that neither her husband nor Dromio has returned for

dinner. Gently, Luciana tries to soothe the impatience and anger of her shrewish sister. Dromio comes in and tells of his encounter with Antipholus (of Syracuse), as a result of which he has concluded that his master is "stark mad." Adriana angrily commands Dromio to go back and fetch her husband. Luciana urges patience on Adriana, who declares that Antipholus mistreats and neglects her and must be showing attention to another woman. "How many fond fools serve mad jealousy!" Luciana comments.

II,ii. The Mart [Market]

Antipholus of Syracuse, having found his money safe at the Centaur, meets his own Dromio, who has come looking for his master. He chides the servant for having denied possession of the gold and for having called him to dinner. While the master and servant converse, Adriana and Luciana approach.

Believing that she has met her husband, Adriana roundly accuses Antipholus of Syracuse of immorality and of mistreating her. He protests that he does not know her and declares that he has been in Ephesus no longer than two hours. Mistaking Dromio of Syracuse for their own servant, Luciana and Adriana insist that they sent him to look for his master. Since this corresponds with the conversation that Antipholus had with Dromio of Ephesus, he accuses his own servant of lying. Persuaded that they are in a fairyland ruled by sorcery or that they are dreaming, Antipholus and Dromio of Syracuse accompany Luciana and Adriana home for dinner.

III,i. In Front of the House of Antipholus of Ephesus

Antipholus of Ephesus is chatting with Angelo, a goldsmith, and Balthazar, a merchant. Angry because Dromio of Ephesus has complained of the recent abuse he received from Antipholus of Syracuse (I,ii), he accuses his servant of being an ass. Antipholus invites Balthazar to dine with him, but when they attempt to enter the house they find the door locked against them. Inside, Dromio of Syracuse follows Adriana's instructions and refuses to admit anyone. Antipholus and Dromio of Ephesus make such a commotion that Luce and Adriana call down from the upper floor. Unable to see the men in the street, they fail to recognize them and order them away. Puzzled and enraged, Antipholus and Dromio vow to punish those who are barring them from their own house. Determined to break open the door, Antipholus orders Dromio to bring him a crowbar. Balthazar reminds Antipholus of the risk of rousing the curiosity and gossip of the public and implores him to "depart in patience." He then invites Antipholus, Dromio, and Angelo to accompany him to the Tiger Inn for dinner, suggesting that Antipholus can return later at a more quiet hour to learn the reason for his exclusion. Antipholus agrees, commenting that at the Tiger he will find "a wench of excellent discourse" about whom Adriana has often chided him. Resolved to spite Andiana, Antipholus directs Angelo to bring him a gold chain which he will present to the hostess of another inn, the Porpentine. Angelo promises to meet Antipholus there.

III,ii. In Front of the House of Antipholus of Ephesus

Luciana is shaming Antipholus of Syracuse for having forgotten his relationship as husband of Adriana and for having tried to woo her, his sister-in-law. In vain Antipholus protests, "Your weeping sister is no wife of mine," as indeed she is not. With growing ardor he professes his love for Luciana. Greatly distressed, Luciana leaves him to fetch Adriana.

No sooner has Luciana left than Dromio of Syracuse comes running from the house. In answer to his master's inquiry, Dromio says that he is fleeing the advances of Nell (Luce), whom he describes in unflattering terms. Nell has mistaken him for her fellow servant, Dromio of Ephesus, and claims him as her fiancé. After hearing his man out, Antipholus of Syracuse tells him that they will leave Ephesus as quickly as possible, and observes,

> If every one knows us, and we know none,
> 'Tis time, I think, to trudge, pack, and be gone.

Still dreading Nell's possessiveness, Dromio runs away. While Antipholus muses on his dislike for Adriana and his newly awakened love for Luciana, Angelo appears with the gold chain ordered by Antipholus of Ephesus.

Angelo argues that Antipholus, whom he mistakes for his brother, has commissioned the chain and thrusts it upon him, saying that he will call at supper time to collect the money for it. Bewildered, Antipholus accepts the ornament, thinking

> there's no man is so vain
> That would refuse so fair an offer'd chain.

IV,i. A Public Place

The Second Merchant half-apologetically tells Angelo, the goldsmith, that necessity compels him to collect a debt from Angelo.

Facing immediate arrest if he does not pay the Second Merchant, Angelo suggests that they walk to the house of Antipholus, who owes him an identical amount for the chain. At this instant they meet Antipholus and Dromio of Ephesus as they come from the house of the Courtesan. On seeing Angelo, Antipholus sends Dromio to procure a rope which he will present to Adriana as a gift for locking him out of his own house.

Antipholus then chides Angelo for having failed to bring the chain as he had promised. Confident that he has already delivered the merchandise to Antipholus in person (III,ii), Angelo itemizes the cost of the chain and requests Antipholus to pay the sum to the Second Merchant. Antipholus of Ephesus naturally does not have the chain and indignantly refuses to pay anything until he receives it. Angered by his arrest at the behest of the Merchant, Angelo demands that the Officer arrest Antipholus on a similar charge of debt.

As the men continue quarreling, Dromio of Syracuse appears and, mistaking Antipholus of Ephesus for his own master, tells him that he has chartered a ship on which they can leave at once. Threatening to chastise Dromio for this mad insolence, Antipholus directs him to go to Adriana and bring a purse of ducats for his bail. Reluctant to face Nell again, Dromio departs to carry out instructions from the man he thinks to be Antipholus of Syracuse.

IV,ii. The House of Antipholus of Ephesus

Luciana is describing to Adriana the way in which Antipholus of Syracuse made love to her. Both sisters assume, of course, that Luciana's suitor was Antipholus of Ephesus, Adriana's husband. In the midst of their conversation, Dromio of Syracuse enters and requests the purse of ducats (IV,i). Learning of her husband's arrest, Adriana asks Luciana to fetch the money and give it to Dromio, although she is greatly surprised that Antipholus is in debt.

IV,iii. The Mart [Market]

Puzzled by the fact that everyone who meets him salutes him as a "well-acquainted friend," Antipholus of Syracuse concludes that his imagination is playing tricks on him or that "Lapland sorcerers inhabit" Ephesus. Dromio of Syracuse, returning with the money he has received from Adriana, is surprised to find Antipholus released from his arrest for debt. Their efforts to explain matters lead only to more confusion. Antipholus decides that "The fellow is distract, and so am I." At this point the Courtesan accosts Antipholus and

demands either her ring or the gold chain. Antipholus of Syracuse
knows nothing of the woman, curses her, and orders her to depart.
He and Dromio leave her. Convinced that Antipholus, whom she
mistakes for his brother, is insane, the Courtesan resolves to explain
the matter to Adriana and tell her that Antipholus took the ring by
force, "For forty ducats is too much to lose."

IV,iv. A Street

Antipholus of Ephesus assures the Officer that he will not attempt
to break his arrest because he is confident that Adriana will send the
ducats for his bail. Dromio of Ephesus now returns with the rope
(IV,i); he denies knowledge of the five hundred ducats for bail
money, and Antipholus beats him. As Antipholus chastises Dromio
for a second time, Adriana, Luciana, the Courtesan, and Pinch
appear.

Adriana, persuaded by her husband's words and actions that evil
spirits have possessed him, urges Doctor Pinch to cast out the demons.
Striking Pinch, who begins his exorcism, Antipholus insists that he
himself is completely sane. Attempts by Antipholus and Dromio to
explain all that has passed serve merely to make Adriana and Pinch
more certain of the master's and servant's present insanity.

Alarmed by the violence of Antipholus, Adriana and Pinch summon help in order to bind him. As Antipholus struggles, the Officer
commands the group to leave the prisoner in his custody. On Pinch's
advice, the men seize and tie Dromio. Upon Adriana's assurance that
she will discharge her husband's debt, the Officer permits the con-
veyance of Antipholus to Adriana's care. Men bear Antipholus and
Dromio away.

While Adriana is discussing her husband's debts with the Officer
in the presence of Luciana and the Courtesan, Antipholus of Syracuse, accompanied by his own Dromio, appears waving his drawn
rapier. Thinking that the insane Antipholus and Dromio of Ephesus
have broken from their confinement and returned, Adriana and her
companions flee in terror. Antipholus of Syracuse declares that he and
his servant will leave Ephesus as speedily as they can.

V,i. A Street in Front of a Priory

Angelo is apologizing to the Second Merchant for the delay in
paying him, but he expresses confidence in the integrity of Antipholus
of Ephesus, from whom he must collect for the gold chain. While
they talk, Antipholus and Dromio of Syracuse appear. Seeing that

Antipholus is wearing the chain, Angelo mistakes him for his twin and chides him for having denied receipt of the chain. When Antipholus protests that he has denied nothing, the Second Merchant supports Angelo's accusation. Infuriated, Antipholus and the Merchant draw their weapons as Adriana, Luciana, the Courtesan, and others approach.

Supposing that she sees her husband and his servant, Adriana exhorts her attendants to avoid hurting the insane men but at the same time to bind them and take them to her house. On Dromio's advice, he and his master dash into the Priory for sanctuary.

Alerted by the uproar, the Lady Abbess emerges to inquire its cause. Adriana explains that for the past week her husband has appeared distracted, the seizure reaching a peak on this afternoon. Under continued questioning by the Abbess, Adriana admits that she suspects her husband of infidelity and that she has nagged him unceasingly about it at meals, in bed, and at other times. On hearing this, the Abbess places the responsibility for Antipholus's madness on Adriana, pointing out that sleeplessness, indigestion, and constant reproof can "mad or man or beast." She says,

> The venom clamours of a jealous woman
> Poisons more deadly than a mad dog's tooth.
> ....
>   . . . thy jealous fits
> Have scar'd thy husband from the use of wits.

Adriana confesses the justice of the Abbess's rebuke but asks that she receive custody of her husband, or failing this, that the Abbess permit her to enter the Priory and nurse him. The Abbess refuses all of Adriana's requests, declaring that she herself will minister to him and restore him to his right mind.

On Luciana's advice, Adriana resolves to plead with Solinus, Duke of Ephesus, to intervene and restore her husband to her by force. Hearing this, the Second Merchant says that it is almost five o'clock, the hour when Solinus will arrive to supervise the beheading of old Aegeon.

Arriving with Aegeon, the Headsman, and other officers, Solinus once more proclaims that if any person will pay Aegeon's fine, the old man may live. At this moment Adriana sues the Duke for justice against the Abbess. After listening to her account of what has happened, Solinus says that he will review the matter at once.

Suddenly a messenger runs up with the news that Antipholus and

Dromio of Ephesus have broken their bonds, attacked Doctor Pinch, and are threatening violence on Adriana. Thinking that her husband and his servant are in the Priory, Adriana charges the Messenger with lying, but at this moment Antipholus and Dromio of Ephesus arrive on the scene.

While Antipholus of Ephesus begs the Duke's assistance, Aegeon mistakes him and Dromio of Ephseus for their twin brothers. Utterly bewildered by the conflicting accounts and explanations of Antipholus, Adriana, Angelo, the Second Merchant, and the Courtesan, the Duke concludes that they are all dazed or "stark mad" and sends for the Abbess.

In the meantime, Aegeon addresses Antipholus and Dromio of Ephesus by their correct names, but they insist that they recognize neither his face nor his voice. Unable to believe that they could have forgotten him during seven years of separation, Aegeon charges his son with being ashamed to acknowledge him in his misery. Antipholus stoutly maintains that he never saw his father in his lifetime, and the Duke testifies that Antipholus has not visited Syracuse for the past twenty years.

At this point the Abbess arrives with Antipholus and Dromio of Syracuse. While Adriana believes that she sees two husbands and the Duke thinks that one Antipholus is the Genius (attendant spirit) of the other, Antipholus and Dromio of Syracuse recognize Aegeon. On hearing the name Aegeon and perceiving that the old man is her long-lost husband, the Abbess says that she will loose his bonds and identifies herself as his wife Aemilia. Briefly the Abbess relates how Corinthian fishermen, after the rescue at sea, seized the twins and left her with the men of Epidamnum.

In the midst of a happy family reunion, the various charges and countercharges resolve themselves. Antipholus of Ephesus acknowledges himself to be Adriana's husband, and Antipholus of Syracuse eagerly tells Luciana that he will now prove his protestations of love. The Antipholuses offer to pay the ransom for their father's life, but the Duke remits the fine. The Abbess, having reached the end of thirty-three years of lonely separation from her husband and sons, invites the entire company "to a gossips' feast" in the Priory.

Left to themselves, the two Antipholuses and the two Dromios discover that they have as much difficulty in identifying the proper master and servant as other people have had. Jesting with each other, the two Dromios say that they will draw lots to determine which is the elder brother.

THE TAMING OF THE SHREW
[1593–   ?]

CHARACTERS

A Lord.
CHRISTOPHER
  SLY, a tinker.
Hostess, Page
  [Bartholomew],
Players,
Huntsmen, and
Servants.
} Persons in the Induction.

BAPTISTA MINOLA, a gentleman of Padua.

VINCENTIO, a merchant of Pisa.

LUCENTIO [CAMBIO], son to *Vincentio*, in love with *Bianca*.

PETRUCHIO, a gentleman of Verona, suitor to *Katherina*.

GREMIO,
HORTENSIO
  [LICIO],
} suitors to *Bianca*.

TRANIO,
BIONDELLO,
} servants to *Lucentio*.

GRUMIO,
CURTIS,
} servants to *Petruchio*.

A Pedant.

KATHERINA,
  the shrew,
BIANCA,
} daughters to *Baptista*.

A Widow.

Tailor, Haberdasher, and Servants [Nathaniel, Joseph, Nicholas, Philip, Walter, Sugarsop, Gregory, Gabriel, Peter, Adam, Ralph].

Scene: *Padua, and Petruchio's House in the Country*

Induction, i. In Front of an Alehouse on a Heath

When Christopher Sly refuses to pay for the glasses he has broken, the Hostess leaves to fetch a constable. Sly falls asleep on the ground, where a Lord and his hunting party discover him. Noting Sly's drunkenness, the Lord directs his attendants to transport the unconscious beggar to a luxurious chamber, array him in elegant clothes, and furnish him with a delicious banquet and music. When Sly comes to his senses, they are to treat him as if he were "a mighty lord." Serv-

11

ants carry Sly out as a trumpet sounds the approach of a band of players.

Welcoming the strolling actors, the Lord tells them that he wishes them to produce a play for his guest that evening. The Lord then sends one of his servants to arrange for the Page, Bartholomew, to dress like a lady and lavish attention on the drunken Sly. Pleased with the elaborate prank he has planned, the Lord departs so that he may check the enthusiasm of his men if they carry the joke too far.

Induction, ii. A Bedroom in the Lord's House

Sly, protesting that he is a humble tinker by profession and that the Lord and his attendants are trying to make him mad, decides that he is not asleep and that he is a "lord indeed." Persuaded that he has been out of his mind for fifteen years, Sly accepts the services proffered him and thanks the Lord for his "good amends." After the Page, disguised as a lady, enters and converses with Sly, the old beggar dismisses his attendants and orders his "Madam wife" to bed with him. His alleged "Lady" pleads for delay on the grounds that physicians fear the return of his recent illness. Sly agrees that he would be loath to fall into his dreams again. A Messenger announces the arrival of the actors to present "a pleasant comedy" which the doctors have prescribed to expedite Sly's recovery. Sly and his assumed wife prepare to witness the play, which follows.

I,i. Padua. A Public Place

Lucentio, son of the prosperous merchant Vincentio, has come from Pisa to Padua to continue his study in philosophy. His man, Tranio, advises him to lighten his serious education with frequent excursions into Ovid, music, and similar subjects. Lucentio approves Tranio's counsel and wishes that his other servant, Biondello, would join them so that they could secure suitable lodgings. Lucentio and Tranio stand aside as Baptista and his two daughters enter. Accompanying them are Gremio, a foolish and feeble old man, and Hortensio, both suitors for the hand of Bianca.

Baptista informs Gremio and Hortensio that he will not betroth Bianca to anyone until he arranges a marriage for Katherina, his elder daughter. He is willing for either Gremio or Hortensio to court Katherina, but, because of her sharp tongue and shrewish manners, neither man is interested in her. In asides, Tranio comments on Katherina's frowardness, and Lucentio praises Bianca's mild behavior, sobriety, and appearance. Sending Bianca into the house, Baptista asks Hortensio and Gremio to recommend tutors in "music, instruments, and poetry" for his younger daughter. He then goes to talk with Bianca, Katherina following him.

Gremio, somewhat pessimistic about his prospects as a suitor in light of what Baptista has said, tells Hortensio that he will try to locate a suitable teacher for Bianca. Hortensio suggests that he and Gremio join forces in an attempt to persuade some man to marry Katherina, thus making Bianca eligible for their rival courtship. Temporarily in league with each other, they leave.

Lucentio declares to Tranio that he has fallen helplessly in love with Bianca. In order to be near her, he will apply for the post of tutor. When Tranio warns that someone must play the role of Vincentio's son in Padua, Lucentio insists that Tranio impersonate him. Obediently Tranio agrees, and they exchange clothes. Biondello comes up and inquires about their change of dress. Lucentio tells Biondello that Tranio is wearing his master's apparel to protect him from arrest for murder. Biondello consents to cooperate in the deception, and Lucentio orders Tranio to present himself as another suitor for Bianca.

At this point Christopher Sly's companions accuse him of nodding and not paying attention to the play. He insists that it is "a very excellent piece of work," but wishes " 'twere done."

I,ii. Padua. In Front of Hortensio's House

Petruchio arrives in Padua to visit friends, particularly Hortensio. Boisterously, he wrings Grumio's ears and forces the servant to knock on Hortensio's door. Hortensio appears, welcomes them, and mediates the quarrel between them. To Hortensio's inquiry as to what brings him to Padua, Petruchio replies that he has inherited the estate of his recently deceased father, Antonio, and has come to seek a wife and see the world.

Immediately Hortensio says that he can introduce Petruchio to a very rich, "shrewd, ill-favour'd wife," but adds that Petruchio is too much his friend to be served in this fashion. Petruchio declares that if the woman is wealthy he cares not how foul, old, or shrewish she may be. Seeing that Petruchio is apparently serious, Hortensio continues what he "broach'd in jest" and describes Baptista and Katherina in greater detail. Petruchio says that he will not sleep until he meets this daughter of an intimate friend of his late father. Confessing his love for Bianca and explaining Baptista's isolation of her

until "Katherine the curst" secures a husband, Hortensio asks
Petruchio to introduce him disguised as a music master into the
Minola household.

When Gremio enters with Lucentio, who pretends to be a schoolmaster, Hortensio, Grumio, and Petruchio stand aside. Gremio is
engaging Lucentio (who calls himself Cambio) to double as Bianca's
tutor and his go-between. Hortensio steps forward, tells Gremio that
he has secured a music teacher for Bianca, and introduces Petruchio
as a prospective suitor for Katherina. Gremio and Hortensio agree
to bear the expenses of Petruchio's wooing. At this point Tranio
(impersonating Lucentio) and Biondello join the group. Asking
directions to Baptista's house, Tranio declares his intention of wooing Bianca in the face of Gremio's and Hortensio's objections.
Finally the three rivals suspend their bickering to abet Petruchio.
Tranio suggests that they drink to Bianca's health

> And do as adversaries do in law—
> Strive mightily, but eat and drink as friends.

II,i. Padua. Baptista's House

Katherina has tied Bianca's hands and is tormenting her to learn
the name of her favorite suitor. Baptista comes in, releases Bianca,
and rebukes Katherina, who says that Bianca's silence flouts her.
She tries to attack her sister again, berates her father for his favori-
tism to Bianca, and follows her sister out.

Now Gremio, Lucentio, Petruchio, Hortensio, Tranio, and Biondello enter. Petruchio introduces himself to Baptista and presents
Hortensio as Licio, a Mantuan "cunning in music and the mathe-
matics." Gremio then recommends Lucentio as Cambio, a young
scholar in "Greek, Latin, and other languages." Tranio presents himself as Lucentio, a suitor for the hand of Bianca, and produces a
lute and packet of books for Bianca to use in her studies. Baptista
extends a warm welcome to all and sends Hortensio to instruct
Katherina in music and Lucentio to tutor Bianca in languages.

Eager to further his wooing of Katherina, Petruchio negotiates
a satisfactory marriage contract with Baptista on condition that
he win the approval of the high-spirited girl. Petruchio confidently
discounts Katherina's reputation for shrewishness despite Baptista's
friendly warning. At this instant, Hortensio reports that Katherina
has broken the lute over his head and that he can do nothing with

her. Petruchio acclaims Katherina's spirit, and Baptista tells Hortensio to continue lessons with Bianca. Baptista promises to send Katherina to Petruchio, who resolves to praise whatever she says or does.

Refusing to address Katherina by her full name, Petruchio persists in calling her Kate and returns insult for insult in the conversation that follows. In fury she strikes him, but Petruchio continues to pretend that he finds her "soft and affable" and tells her that, whether she wishes or not, he is going to marry her. Reappearing with Gremio and Tranio, Baptista asks Petruchio how he is faring. Petruchio answers that it is impossible that he should "speed amiss" and tells Baptista to make preparations for the wedding feast. Receiving the paternal blessing, Petruchio says that he has to go to Venice and that he and Katherina will marry on Sunday.

Anticipating the imminent marriage of Katherina, Gremio and Tranio begin to wrangle with Baptista over their claims to Bianca. Baptista says that he will give Bianca to the suitor who can provide the greatest dower. In an extravagant listing of wealth and resources, Tranio outbids Gremio for Bianca. Baptista decides that Bianca will marry Tranio on the Sunday following Kate's wedding with Petruchio, if Tranio can guarantee his offer. Otherwise Bianca will marry Gremio.

Gremio warns Tranio that his father will hardly prove so rash as to furnish him with the dower he has pledged. Alone, Tranio congratulates himself on having put down Gremio with his impersonation, but he faces the necessity of producing someone to represent Vincentio who will, in the manner of a rich and indulgent parent, support his promises.

III,i. Padua. Baptista's House

Lucentio (as Cambio, the scholar) and Hortensio (as Licio, the music master) are quarreling as to which one shall have priority in teaching Bianca. Bianca tells Hortensio to tune his instrument while Lucentio continues his lecture on Ovid. Under pretext of construing the Latin poetry, Lucentio whispers to Bianca who he is and explains that Tranio is impersonating him in order to beguile Gremio. Also whispering, Bianca replies that she neither knows Lucentio nor trusts him, cautions against being overheard by the music master, and tells him neither to presume nor to despair. When his turn comes, Hortensio employs his lesson in music to reveal himself to Bianca and plead for her love, but he receives no encouragement. A Messenger from Baptista summons Bianca to assist in preparing for Kate's wedding on the morrow.

III,ii. Padua. In Front of Baptista's House

In the presence of the wedding party, Baptista asks Tranio (as Lucentio) what he thinks of Petruchio's failure to appear for the ceremony. Katherina, denouncing Petruchio as a "frantic fool," says that she will be a laughingstock. Tranio tries to reassure father and daughter, but Katherina retires in tears. Biondello enters and reports that Petruchio, Grumio accompanying him, is approaching on an old nag and that he has ridiculously and outrageously arrayed himself in an assortment of castoff garments and weapons.

Petruchio enters with Grumio and demands his lovely bride. He dismisses questions about his tardiness and appearance by saying that it suffices that he has kept his word and that Kate is marrying him and not his clothes. He and Grumio hasten to greet the bride, Baptista, Gremio, and attendants following them.

In the meantime, Tranio tells Lucentio that they must find someone to play the part of Vincentio. Lucentio remarks that except for Hortensio's watchful presence, he would elope with Bianca; Tranio assures him that they will find means of overcoming all obstacles to his courtship.

Gremio returns to describe the "mad marriage." Petruchio shocked the priest and cuffed him, spoke his vows with blasphemous oaths, terrified the bride, threw wine-sops in the sexton's face, and kissed his wife with "a clamorous smack." Entering with the wedding party, Petruchio thanks his friends and guests but says that business prevents his staying for the nuptial feast they have prepared. Petruchio steadfastly rejects all pleas that he stay, even Katherina's. Pretending to protect his wife from the onlookers, Petruchio orders Grumio to draw his sword and cover their withdrawal as he leads Kate away.

While all make jocular comments about the departing couple, Baptista invites the party to the marriage feast and says that Tranio (as Lucentio) will occupy Petruchio's place and Bianca the bride's.

IV,i. Petruchio's Country House

Complaining of the cold, Grumio enters to prepare for the arrival of the bride and groom. He calls Curtis and orders him to make a fire. Learning that supper is ready, the house clean, the servants suitably dressed, Grumio tells Curtis how Petruchio beat him when Kate's horse fell in the mud beneath her and how Petruchio abandoned his bride, forcing her to wade out of the mire by herself. Grumio then inspects the servants, who have tidied the house and themselves.

Entering with Katherina, Petruchio berates the servants for their slipshod appearance and derelict welcome. Finding fault with all of them, Petruchio orders his supper. He continues to curse and abuse his servants until Katherina pleads in their behalf. When his food appears, Petruchio pronounces it burnt and unfit to eat and throws it and the dishes at the servants, whom he denounces. Kate remonstrates that the meat was satisfactorily cooked, but Petruchio declares that they will fast on their wedding night and conducts her to the bridal chamber.

Sagely the servants discuss Petruchio's method of chastening Katherina with her own "humour." Petruchio returns and in a soliloquy discloses his strategy of taming his shrewish wife with hunger and sleeplessness, all the while pretending that "all is done in reverend care of her."

IV,ii. Padua. In Front of Baptista's House

Tranio and Hortensio, observing Bianca and Lucentio (in his disguise as Cambio) together, realize that Bianca has given her heart to her tutor. Hortensio admits his true identity to Tranio and says that he is neither Licio nor a musician. Tranio suggests that they pledge to each other that neither will woo Bianca again, and Hortensio agrees to forswear her. Still believing Tranio to be Lucentio, Hortensio tells him and Bianca that he will marry a wealthy widow and takes his leave. Tranio then tells Bianca that he, too, has forsworn her.

Biondello comes with the news that he has found a Pedant who may prove a likely candidate to impersonate Vincentio. Lucentio and Bianca depart as the Pedant arrives. Ascertaining that the Pedant comes from Mantua, Tranio introduces himself as the son of Vincentio of Pisa and tells the Pedant that the Duke of Padua has decreed the death penalty on any Mantuan found in the city. Tranio then suggests that the Pedant can save his life if he will assume the role of Vincentio and "pass assurance of a dow'r in marriage" between Tranio and Baptista's daughter. This business the Pedant gratefully undertakes.

IV,iii. Petruchio's House

Katherina is pleading with Grumio to bring her something to eat, but the servant makes objection to one dish after another. In frustration, Katherina beats him as Petruchio and Hortensio enter with food which Petruchio immediately threatens to remove, but Kate begs him to leave it. Hortensio offers to eat with her. In a whisper, Petruchio asks his friend to devour all the food while a Tailor and a Haberdasher divert Katherina's attention with their measuring and fitting. Although the cap and gown satisfy Kate, Petruchio will purchase neither. Dismissing the designers with pretended rage, Petruchio tells his still famished wife that they will return to her father's "in these honest mean habiliments."

IV,iv. Padua. In Front of Baptista's House

Tranio (as Lucentio) and Biondello introduce the Pedant as Vincentio to Baptista, whom the real Lucentio accompanies in the role of Cambio. Reassured by the Pedant's promise of an ample dower, Baptista consents to wed Bianca to the supposed Lucentio. When the others have departed to carry the news to Bianca, Biondello advises Lucentio to elope with Bianca and marry her at Saint Luke's Church, where the priest will wait at his command.

IV,v. A Public Road

Petruchio urges Katherina to continue their journey under the bright moonlight. When Katherina starts to argue that the sun and not the moon is shining, Hortensio begs her to agree to whatever outlandish statement Petruchio makes. Kate meekly submits, and when the three resume their travel they encounter the real Vincentio, whom Petruchio commands Kate to greet as a "budding virgin, fair and fresh and sweet." After she complies, Petruchio asks her if she does not see that Vincentio is actually "a man, old, wrinkled, faded, withered." Much bewildered, Vincentio pardons their "strange encounter" and, identifying himself, tells them that he is going to Padua to visit Lucentio. Petruchio and Hortensio inform Vincentio that his son has married Katherina's sister, invite the old man to join them, and they continue their way together.

V,i. Padua. In Front of Lucentio's House

Lucentio, Bianca, and Biondello start for Saint Luke's Church as Gremio wonders why Cambio has not appeared. Petruchio and his group enter, and Vincentio knocks at Lucentio's door. When the Pedant looks out of the window, Petruchio bids him tell Lucentio that his father has arrived from Pisa. Playing his role faithfully, the Pedant insists that he is the real parent. Biondello, returning from the marriage of Lucentio and Bianca, denies acquaintance with his old master Vincentio, who chases the servant off with blows.

While Petruchio and Katherina stand aside, the Pedant, Baptista, Tranio, and others come to investigate the commotion. When Tranio and the Pedant persist in their impersonations, Vincentio concludes that Tranio has murdered Lucentio. Tranio calls for an Officer and instructs him to convey Vincentio to jail. Baptista agrees to this move, but Gremio warns him against having a part in such rash action because he thinks that he has recognized Vincentio. Confused by Tranio, whom he believes to be Lucentio, Gremio declines to swear to his identification, and Baptista again orders Vincentio to jail.

At this moment Biondello, Bianca, and Lucentio appear. As Lucentio kneels to receive his father's pardon, Biondello, Tranio, and the Pedant scamper off. Lucentio then explains to Vincentio, Baptista, and Gremio all that has happened. Katherina suggests to Petruchio that they follow the others "to see the end of this ado." He agrees on condition that she overcome her embarrassment and kiss him in public, which she does.

V,ii. Lucentio's House

All, including Hortensio and his "loving widow," are feasting. While they are teasing and bantering one another, Petruchio stakes Hortensio a hundred marks that Katherina will get the better of the Widow in jesting. After the three wives depart, Baptista declares that he thinks Petruchio has married "the veriest shrew of all." Petruchio gallantly defends his Kate and suggests,

> Let's each one send unto his wife;
> And he whose wife is most obedient
> To come at first when he doth send for her,
> Shall win the wager which we will propose.

Each husband agrees to stake a hundred crowns on his own wife, Lucentio declining Baptista's offer to underwrite half of the wager on Bianca.

Lucentio sends Biondello to "bid" Bianca come, but the servant quickly returns with word that she "is busy" and "cannot come." Hortensio then directs Biondello to "entreat" his wife to come to him "forthwith." In a moment Biondello reports that Hortensio's wife fears some joke and "bids" him come to her.

Professing impatience with these manifestations of wifely disobedience, Petruchio orders Grumio to go to Katherina and "Say I command her come to me." While Hortensio is predicting that Kate will refuse, she enters and meekly asks Petruchio what he wishes of her. Petruchio tells her to fetch Bianca and the Widow and to thrash them forth if they hesitate. Amazed and gratified to see how successful Petruchio has been in taming the shrewish Katherina, Baptista adds twenty thousand pounds to her dowry.

When Katherina escorts Bianca and Hortensio's wife into the room, Petruchio commands her to remove her cap and step on it and then to lecture Bianca and the other bride on their proper duty and conduct as wives. Pleased with her compliance and execution of his commands, Petruchio exclaims,

> Why, there's a wench! Come on, and kiss me, Kate.

THE TWO GENTLEMEN OF VERONA
[1594–1595]

CHARACTERS

DUKE OF MILAN, father to *Silvia*.

VALENTINE, { the Two
PROTEUS, { Gentlemen.

ANTONIO, father to *Proteus*.

THURIO, a foolish rival to *Valentine*.

EGLAMOUR, agent for *Silvia* in her escape.

HOST, where *Julia* lodges.

OUTLAWS, with *Valentine*.

SPEED, a clownish servant to *Valentine*.

LAUNCE, the like to *Proteus*.

PANTHINO, servant to *Antonio*.

JULIA [SEBASTIAN], beloved of *Proteus*.

SILVIA, beloved of *Valentine*.

LUCETTA, waiting woman to Julia.

Servants.

Musicians.

Scene: *Verona; Milan; a Forest*

I,i. Verona. An Open Place

Proteus has been trying to persuade Valentine to remain in Verona. Valentine says that he would rather Proteus accompanied him on his tour of the world, but he knows that his friend is reluctant to leave his sweetheart Julia. Finding Valentine steadfast in his determination to depart, Proteus bids him adieu and says, "Upon some book I love I'll pray for thee." Valentine observes that this book will be "some shallow story of deep love" and accuses Proteus of foolishly having allowed love to enslave him. The friends part amicably, Valentine urging Proteus to write him in Milan. After Valentine has gone, Proteus comments to himself that Valentine leaves his friend to seek honor whereas he, Proteus, forsakes all his acquaintances, neglects his studies, and wastes his time because of his love for Julia.

At this moment, Speed enters, seeking his master, Valentine. Telling Speed that Valentine has already started for Milan, Proteus inquires if Speed has faithfully delivered his letter to Julia. Eager for news of his sweetheart, Proteus pumps Speed for Julia's reply, but Speed cannily evades answering until Proteus has given him a sixpence tip. Then Speed reports that Julia said nothing at all upon receipt of the letter; he adds that henceforth, in view of the small reward, Proteus may carry his own letters. Proteus dismisses Speed and reflects that he must find a better messenger.

I,ii. Verona. The Garden of Julia's House

Julia and Lucetta are discussing Julia's suitors. In reply to her mistress's questions, Lucetta says that she thinks Proteus the best of all but does not give any basis for her opinion beyond "a woman's reason:/I think him so because I think him so." Confessing that Proteus alone of her suitors has not proposed to her, Julia admits that she would like to know his intentions. Immediately Lucetta hands Julia the letter which she has received in Julia's name from Speed. Julia chides Lucetta for having accepted the note and commands her to return it. After Lucetta leaves, Julia blames herself for having dismissed her waiting woman and criticizes Lucetta for not having forced her to read it, "Since maids, in modesty, say 'no' to that/Which they would have the profferer construe 'ay'!" Quickly she decides to ask Lucetta's forgiveness and calls her back.

While she jests with Lucetta, Julia takes the letter, again loses her patience, and tears it into pieces. When Lucetta retires, Julia collects the scraps and reads them, folds them together, and embraces them. Lucetta comes to call Julia to dinner and gathers the fragments of the letter, which Julia now pretends to regard as worthless.

I,iii. Verona. Antonio's House

Panthino tells his master of the concern of Proteus's uncle for his nephew. Antonio agrees that Proteus ought to leave home and seek experience in the world. In response to Antonio's request for advice, Panthino suggests that Proteus join Valentine as an attendant on the Emperor (i.e., Duke) in Milan. Antonio approves the plan just as Proteus enters with a letter from Julia. When his father inquires about the letter, Proteus tells Antonio that it is from Valentine urging him to come to Milan. Antonio asks Proteus what he wishes to do, and the young man says that he will follow his father's will in the matter. Antonio dismays Proteus by telling him that he will depart the next day. After Antonio and Panthino leave, Proteus comments to himself that his attempt to conceal Julia's authorship of the letter has backfired because now he must leave Verona. Panthino returns to summon Proteus to Antonio.

II,i. Milan. The Duke's Palace

Speed hands Valentine a glove which Valentine claims as a token from Silvia—"Sweet ornament that decks a thing divine!" When Valentine asks him if he knows Madam Silvia, Speed humorously charges Valentine with being in love and describes the many symptoms of love that Valentine has unwittingly displayed. Finally Valentine admits that he stands "affected" to her and that at her request he has written some lines "to one she loves." Silvia appears, and Valentine modestly gives her the letter. Silvia reads the paper, commends it, but insists on returning it to Valentine. Valentine says that he will write another, and Silvia comments that if the second letter pleases him he may keep it for his pains. She leaves, and Speed shrewdly explains to his master that Silvia has cleverly maneuvered Valentine into composing her love messages to himself. "Herself hath taught her love himself to write unto her lover," Speed says.

II,ii. Verona. Julia's House

Julia and Proteus, taking leave of each other, exchange rings as symbols of their love, sealing their affection with a kiss. Pledging his faith to her, Proteus sadly clasps her hands and bids her not to weep. Julia departs, and Panthino comes to inform Proteus that his party is waiting for him.

II,iii. Verona. A Street

Launce, leading his dog Crab, delivers a comical monologue on his tearful parting from his family. Every member of his household wept and wailed at his departure except Crab, that must "be the sourest-natured dog that lives." Panthino enters and orders Launce to make haste to join his master, Proteus.

II,iv. Milan. The Duke's Palace

Advising his master to give Thurio a hard blow, Speed leaves Valentine and Thurio quarreling in the presence of Silvia, who accuses the two rivals of shooting a "fine volley of words." Silvia commands them to be silent as her father (Duke of Milan) enters with the news that Proteus has arrived in his court. Joyfully Valentine praises the virtues and talents of his friend. Urging Silvia and Thurio to give Proteus a warm welcome, the Duke withdraws.

No sooner has Proteus appeared and exchanged greetings with the others, than a servant summons Silvia to her father. Taking Thurio with her, she follows the servant, leaving Proteus and Valentine to renew their friendship. After politely inquiring about the welfare of mutual friends in Verona, Valentine expressly asks Proteus how his love affair with Julia progresses. Valentine admits that his attitude toward love has changed and confesses that he is madly infatuated with Silvia. They then extol the beauty and superiority of their respective sweethearts.

Proteus inquires if Silvia returns his friend's love, and Valentine confides that he and Silvia are betrothed and are planning to elope. Valentine has already prepared a rope ladder by means of which Silvia may escape from her room, and he asks Proteus to lend him further assistance. Promising to help, Proteus says that he must first remove his belongings from the ship. Valentine hurries off, and Proteus soliloquizes that the charm of Silvia has quelled his love for Julia and lessened his friendship for Valentine. He concludes:

> If I can check my erring love, I will;
> If not, to compass her I'll use my skill.

II,v. Milan. A Street

Speed and Launce meet, exchange news of Valentine and Proteus, trade bawdy and humorous banter, and start for drinks at the alehouse.

II,vi. Milan. The Duke's Palace

Walking alone, Proteus declares his intention of forsaking Julia and betraying Valentine in order to win Silvia for himself. To promote his own cause he will relate Valentine's scheme of eloping with Silvia to the Duke. Anticipating that the enraged Duke will banish Valentine, Proteus will contrive a way to thwart Thurio, whom the Duke favors for Silvia's hand.

II,vii. Verona. Julia's House

Julia is seeking Lucetta's advice as to how she may undertake a journey to see her "loving Proteus." Rejecting Lucetta's counsel that she would do better to await Proteus's return, Julia ask Lucetta to furnish her with a boy's costume in order that she may disguise herself as a page. In spite of her own and Lucetta's misgivings, Julia continues her preparations with complete faith in her lover's sincerity and constancy.

III,i. Milan. The Duke's Palace

Dismissing Thurio, the Duke listens to Proteus's revelation of Valentine's plans to elope with Silvia. The Duke thanks Proteus and says that he has assigned Silvia to "an upper tow'r," locks her door every night, and keeps the key himself. Proteus, who has claimed embarrassment at tattling on his friend, discloses that Valentine will soon arrive with the "corded ladder" in his possession. Proteus retires after receiving the Duke's assurance that Valentine will not learn of his friend's part in exposing the plot.

When Valentine enters, the Duke detains him with a discussion of his hope of arranging a marriage between Silvia and Thurio. The Duke says that because Silvia has proudly and scornfully refused to agree to the match, he has decided to disinherit her without a dowry and to remarry, settling his estate on his second wife. He asks Valentine to tutor him in his courtship.

Misled by the Duke's account of the difficulties he is encountering in wooing, Valentine advises him to use a cord ladder and elope. When the Duke says that he will need the ladder that very night and does not know where to obtain one, Valentine promises to supply one by seven o'clock. As Valentine describes how the Duke may easily conceal the ladder under his cloak, the Duke pulls at Valentine's own cloak and discovers a love note to Silvia and the ladder that Valentine has prepared for her escape. In a rage, the Duke banishes Valentine from his territories and then departs. Despairing of life away from Silvia, Valentine weighs the dangers of emotional death against those of physical death if he remains in Milan.

Proteus arrives with Launce to warn Valentine that the Duke has exiled him by official proclamation. In addition to this, the Duke has consigned Silvia, tearfully interceding for Valentine, "to close prison." Proteus advises Valentine not to waste time in lamenting that which he cannot help, offers to assist him in his departure, and promises to deliver any future letters to Silvia. Valentine asks Launce to send Speed to overtake him and leaves with Proteus.

In a brief soliloquy, Launce reveals that he suspects his master of knavery and starts to read a paper listing the "condition" of the girl with whom he has fallen in love. Speed joins him, and they examine Launce's "cate-log" (catalogue) together. Having mischievously detained Speed in the hope that he will miss his master and be punished, Launce informs him of Valentine's departure.

III,ii. Milan. The Duke's Palace

The Duke is attempting to encourage Thurio, who has received no favors from Silvia since Valentine's banishment. Proteus comes in, and the Duke seeks his advice on how they can induce Silvia to forget Valentine and entertain Thurio's suit. Proteus says that the best way of achieving this will be to slander Valentine with charges of "falsehood, cowardice, and poor descent." Though professing reluctance to be false to his friend, Proteus agrees to undertake the "dispraise" of Valentine. He warns that Silvia will not necessarily esteem Thurio after she abandons her love for Valentine. Nevertheless, he will attempt to promote Thurio's suit. He then advises Thurio to compose love songs for Silvia and to employ musicians to present them beneath her window.

IV,i. A Forest

An outlaw band is preparing to attack approaching travelers. Valentine and Speed fall into the ambush. Despite Speed's fright, Valentine calmly informs the Outlaws that after sixteen months in Milan he has been banished for killing a man in fair fight and is on his way to Verona. One of the Outlaws expresses surprise that Valentine has been punished so severely "for so small a fault," but Valentine comments that he welcomed the sentence. After Valentine says that his early travels and education have given him fluency in languages, the Outlaws invite him to be their commander on pain of instant death if he declines the "courtesy." Valentine accepts their offer on condition that they "do no outrages/On silly women or poor passengers" (i.e., on innocent women or poor travelers).

IV,ii. Milan. Under Silvia's Window

Proteus muses to himself that, since Silvia has rebuffed him with accusations that he has been false to Valentine and to Julia, he must exploit and deceive Thurio as he did his friend. When Thurio arrives with his musicians, Proteus assures him that he, too, loves Silvia, for Thurio's sake. At a distance the Host and Julia (in boy's clothes) listen and chat while the Musicians render the song, "Who is Silvia?" Julia, afraid that Proteus is proving false to her, questions the Host, who quotes Launce's report that Proteus is madly in love with Silvia.

Having received Proteus's assurance that he will plead Thurio's suit with Silvia, Thurio leaves with the Musicians as Julia and the Host continue to watch and listen. When Silvia appears at her window to thank her entertainers, Proteus identifies himself and avows his love for her. Charging Proteus with perjury and disloyalty to Julia and reaffirming her betrothal to Valentine, Silvia spurns and dismisses him. When Proteus begs her to give him her picture for consolation, Silvia promises to send it to him in the morning. Silvia and Proteus withdrawing, Julia, who in several asides has commented on her lover's falseness to her, wakens the Host and inquires where Proteus is living. They leave together.

IV,iii. Milan. Under Silvia's Window

Eglamour calls to Silvia, who appears at her window. Putting her faith in Eglamour, who has vowed perpetual chastity in memory of his deceased sweetheart, Silvia tells him of her father's plan to force her marriage to Thurio, whom she detests. Having heard that Valentine is residing in Mantua, she asks Eglamour if he will escort her there. When he consents to help her, they agree to meet later that evening at Friar Patrick's cell.

IV,iv. Milan. Under Silvia's Window

Launce, leading his dog Crab, soliloquizes on Crab's misbehavior in court society. As he continues talking, Proteus enters with Julia, who is disguised as a page and calls herself Sebastian. In reply to his master's questioning, Launce tells how rascally boys stole the little dog he was taking Silvia as a gift from Proteus. Launce thereupon tried to give her Crab, his own dog. Proteus angrily sends Launce to find the small dog that he lost.

Explaining to Sebastian (Julia) why he has employed him, Proteus commissions the page to deliver a ring to Silvia. Recognizing the ring as the one she gave to Proteus, Julia expresses pity for the sweetheart Proteus has jilted. Proteus's only comment is to give Julia a letter for Silvia as well. He also instructs Julia to remind Silvia that she has promised him her picture. Left alone, Julia bewails her present role as go-between and observes, "Because I love him, I must pity him."

Silvia enters with attendants. When Julia says that she has come for the picture on behalf of Proteus, Silvia sends Ursula, one of her companions, for it. Silvia gives the picture to the page (Julia) with instructions to tell Proteus that Julia would "better fit his chamber than this shadow [picture]." Julia then hands Silvia the letter, which she promptly tears into pieces. Finally Julia tries to give Silvia the ring, but Silvia recognizes it as the one Proteus has described as a love token from Julia, and she declines to accept it. Joy at Silvia's honorable conduct almost betrays Julia into revealing her true identity, but she convinces Silvia of her fondness for Julia and faithfulness to her. Rewarding Sebastian (Julia) for this evidence of loyalty, Silvia departs with her attendants. Remembering Silvia's kindness and virtues, Julia overcomes her jealousy and resolves to take the picture safely to Proteus.

V,i. Milan. An Abbey

Eglamour and Silvia meet at Friar Patrick's cell and set forth on their journey. They are confident that they can evade possible pursuers under cover of the nearby forest.

V,ii. Milan. The Duke's Palace

Proteus, accompanied by Sebastian (Julia), is attempting to persuade Thurio, who is self-conscious about his negroid features, that his suit for Silvia is proceeding satisfactorily. The Duke enters, searching for Eglamour and Silvia. On the basis of a report from Friar Laurence, who has seen the fugitives in the forest, the Duke is certain that Silvia and her escort are on their way to Valentine in Mantua. He invites Proteus and Thurio to join him in pursuit. Thurio agrees, more for revenge on Eglamour than for love of "reckless Silvia." Proteus goes for love of Silvia rather than for hate of Eglamour. Julia also decides to follow in the hope of interfering with Proteus's infatuation.

V,iii. A Forest

Three Outlaws, having captured Silvia but having been unable to overtake the fleeing Eglamour, are conducting her to their captain (Valentine).

V,iv. Another Part of the Forest

Valentine enters, pining for Silvia. Hearing a noise, he reflects that his faithful followers are pursuing another traveler. He comments on the difficulty he has in restraining their violence. Aware of someone's approach, he hides in order to watch what happens.

Proteus, Silvia, and Sebastian (Julia) appear. Proteus has rescued Silvia and seeks "one fair look" for his reward. Repulsing his advances, Silvia says that she would rather have been a breakfast for a hungry lion than be rescued by "false perjur'd Proteus," whom she hates. Reminding Proteus of his inconstancy to Julia, Silvia turns a deaf ear to his declarations of love. Enraged and impassioned by Silvia's rejection, Proteus says that he will force her to yield to his desire. At this moment Valentine emerges from his hiding place, commands Proteus to unhand Silvia, and denounces him as treacherous, "without faith or love."

Smitten by "shame and guilt," Proteus seeks forgiveness, which Valentine immediately grants. Valentine adds, "that my love may appear plain and free,/All that was mine in Silvia I give thee," and Sebastian (Julia) faints.

Recovering from her swoon, Julia says that she neglected to deliver the ring to Silvia and shows the token that Proteus gave her before he left Verona. Upon questioning by Proteus, Julia reveals her identity. Overwhelmed by his sweetheart's evident loyalty, Proteus renounces his love for Silvia and rediscovers his true love for Julia; Valentine declares his and Proteus's friendship restored.

At this instant the Outlaws appear with the Duke and Thurio as captives. Valentine welcomes the Duke graciously but defies Thurio to lay any claim to Silvia. Without argument, the "degenerate and base" Thurio concedes; the Duke, applauding Valentine's spirit, restores his privileges and promises him Silvia's hand in marriage.

Thanking the Duke, Valentine requests an additional favor, which the Duke grants, "whate'er it be." Assuring the Duke of the Outlaws' complete reformation and social rehabilitation, Valentine asks for their pardon and recall from exile. Proclaiming amnesty to everyone, the Duke declares a period of "triumphs, mirth, and rare solemnity." All leave, looking forward to a double marriage and "one mutual happiness."

LOVE'S LABOUR'S LOST [1594–1595]

CHARACTERS

FERDINAND, King of Navarre.

BEROWNE,[1]
LONGAVILLE, } lords attending on the King.
DUMAIN,

BOYET, } lords attending on the *Princess* of France.
MARCADE,

DON ADRIANO DE ARMADO, a fantastical Spaniard.

SIR NATHANIEL, a curate.

HOLOFERNES, a schoolmaster.

[ANTHONY] DULL, a constable.

COSTARD, a clown.

MOTH, page to *Don Armado*.

A Forester.

The PRINCESS of France.

ROSALINE,
MARIA, } ladies attending on the *Princess*.
KATHERINE,

JAQUENETTA, a country wench.

Lords, Attendants, etc.

Scene: *Navarre*

I,i. The King's Park

Ferdinand, eager to make his kingdom of Navarre famous for learning and art, reminds Berowne, Longaville, and Dumain that they have sworn their oaths to spend three years with him in meditation and study. Longaville and Dumain reaffirm their vows and purpose. Berowne, admitting that he has subscribed to live and study with his companions for three years, hesitates to accept certain other restrictions. These are: to see no woman during this period; to eat one meal only on six days in a week and to fast completely on the remaining day; and "to sleep but three hours in the night" and refrain from napping during the day. All of these, he states, "are barren tasks, too hard to keep."

[1] Berowne is the spelling in the earliest editions; some later editors prefer Biron.

Ferdinand and Longaville argue that Berowne has already sworn to all of the conditions, but Berowne says that he swore in jest and turns the tables on them by asking, "What is the end of study?" After much banter and wordplay, Berowne observes,

> So you, to study now it is too late,
> Climb o'er the house to unlock the little gate.

Ferdinand tells Berowne that he may withdraw and go home, whereupon Berowne suddenly declares that he will stay and starts to review the vows.

When he rereads the prohibition against "talking with a woman within the term of three years," Berowne reminds the King that the daughter of the King of France will soon arrive on an official mission. Ferdinand confesses that he had forgotten the visit and declares,

> We must of force dispense with this decree.
> She must lie here on mere necessity.

Quickly Berowne signs the commitment, saying that if he fails to keep his pledges he will plead "mere necessity" as his excuse.

Temporarily freed from their self-imposed restrictions, the King and his attending lords seek amusement in the conversation of Don Armado, "fashion's own knight," a Spaniard famous for his affected manners and extravagant speech. Longaville says that Don Armado and Costard will provide entertainment for the group.

At this moment, Anthony Dull, the constable, appears with Costard, the clown. Dull, whose lisping speech, malapropisms, and name provide clues to his character, bears a letter from Don Armado to the King. To the accompaniment of interruptions and protests from Costard, the Duke reads the letter aloud. In ornate and verbose phrases, Don Armado states that he found Costard consorting with the wench Jaquenetta in the King's park, in violation of the edict recently proclaimed. After Costard confesses in earthy and witty language, the King sentences him to a week's fast on bran and water in the custody of Don Armado. As Ferdinand, Longaville, and Dumain leave to begin their study, Berowne escorts Costard to Don Armado.

I,ii. The Park

Armado enters with Moth, his page. In a conversation glittering with puns and double-entendres, Moth proves himself a worthy pupil of the fantastic Spaniard. Don Armado turns the subject to love and admits to his page that he has succumbed to Jaquenetta's charms. Finding that his "spirit grows heavy in love," Armado orders Moth to sing to him, but the page hesitates as Costard, Dull, and Jaquenetta appear.

Dull commits Costard to the care of Armado. The constable then departs with Jaquenetta, who has been appointed dairy-woman, as Armado protests his love to her. Armado directs Moth to imprison Costard. When they have gone, Armado recalls how Samson, Solomon, and Hercules contested for love, Rejecting rapier, club, and military weapons, Armado resolves to write sonnets in order to express his passion.

II,i. The Park

As the Princess of France arrives with Maria, Katherine, Rosaline, and other attendants, Boyet advises the Princess to exert her utmost charm in conducting negotiations with Ferdinand. Brushing aside Boyet's extravagant compliments, the Princess commands him to take her greetings to the King and learn the monarch's pleasure, because she has heard of his resolution to see no woman for three years. Boyet departs on his errand, and the Princess seeks information from her companions regarding the courtiers attending the King. Maria, Katherine, and Rosaline are so enthusiastic in their praise of Longaville, Dumain, and Berowne that the Princess accuses her ladies of being in love with the three gentlemen they have described. Boyet returns with the news that Ferdinand and his escort are ready to meet the Princess and her party, but that the King plans to lodge his visitors in the field instead of admitting them to his palace.

No sooner has Boyet relayed the message than Ferdinand and his retinue appear and greet the Princess and her company. While Ferdinand and the Princess chat about the unusual welcome he has accorded her and launch their official business, Berowne and Katherine quibble with each other.

Meanwhile Ferdinand and the Princess discuss the possible settlement of an old debt between the King of France and the King of Navarre, involving the province of Aquitaine as security. The Princess insists that her father has repaid half the sum, but Ferdinand is equally positive that neither he nor his father received it. When the Princess says that she can produce the receipts, Boyet says that the packet of state papers has not arrived.

Agreeable to a delay, the King tells the Princess that although his oath precludes his admitting her to the palace, he will entertain her and her companions with fitting hospitality in the park. Berowne and Rosaline have, in the meantime, been exchanging gibes.

As the conferees disperse, Dumain, Longaville, and Berowne slip back privately to learn from Boyet the names of the ladies in whom they are respectively interested. In a merry evaluation of the situation, Boyet tells the Princess and her ladies that he is confident that Ferdinand has fallen in love with the Princess.

III,i. The Park

After a lively exchange with Armado on the subject of wooing, Moth leaves to fetch Costard, by whom the Spaniard wishes to send a letter to Jaquenetta. On Moth's return with Costard, the three engage in more jesting and wordplay. Promising Costard his freedom, Armado gives him the letter to deliver to Jaquenetta. Tipping the clown for this service, Armado takes Moth and departs.

While Costard is reflecting on the miserliness of the three-farthing coin (three-fourths of a penny) that Armado has given him and dignified with the word "remuneration," Berowne approaches and greets him. Berowne likewise has a letter which he wishes Costard to take to Rosaline. "There's thy guerdon," Berowne says, giving the clown a shilling. Deciding that a "guerdon" is worth eleven pence and one farthing more than "remuneration," Costard leaves. In a soliloquy Berowne confesses that, in violation of his prior inclination and vows, he has fallen in love with the dark-eyed Rosaline.

IV,i. The Park

Accompanied by her lords and ladies, the Princess queries a Forester about the hunt and about her own beauty. The Forester answers forthrightly, and the Princess rewards the blunt fellow for his honesty. As they continue chatting, Costard arrives with the announcement that he has a letter from Berowne to Rosaline. On command of the Princess, Boyet examines the letter, which he declares to be addressed to Jaquenetta. The Princess orders Boyet to break the seal and read Don Armado's effusive avowal of love for the country wench. Bewildered by what he has heard, Costard stubbornly maintains that the letter is that which Berowne gave him for Rosaline. The Princess departs with her lords, leaving Boyet, her three ladies, and Costard to jest together.

IV,ii. The Park

Dull, Holofernes, and Sir Nathaniel are discussing the deer hunt with an astonishing assortment of malapropisms, pedantry, and classical and pseudo-classical phrases when Jaquenetta and Costard enter. Jaquenetta asks Sir Nathaniel to read the letter that Costard has given her from Don Armado. This is, of course, the love note that Berowne has composed in verse for Rosaline. Holofernes interposes to amend Sir Nathaniel's reading and, realizing that the letter has miscarried, directs Jaquenetta and Costard to deliver it "into the royal hand of the King." Holofernes invites Sir Nathaniel and Dull to accompany him to dinner where he will criticize the poetry they have just heard.

IV,iii. The Park

Strolling alone with a paper in his hand, Berowne finds satisfaction in the thought that Rosaline has already received his sonnet, and he wishes that his companions were also in love. Seeing the King approaching with a paper, Berowne steps aside and overhears Ferdinand read the poem he has written for the Princess. Scarcely has the King finished and stood to one side when Longaville enters and reads the sonnet he has composed for Maria. To complete the picture, Dumain declaims his lines to Katherine, unaware that the King and his two companions are listening.

When Dumain expresses the wish that his comrades had also deviated from their vows and fallen in love as he has, Longaville advances and tries to shame him. At this the King rebukes both Longaville and Dumain for their offense and warns them that Berowne will mock them for their defection. To the King's chagrin, Berowne now steps forward "to whip hypocrisy," and declares that all of them are "men of inconstancy" and have betrayed him, who alone remains faithful to his oaths. Before Berowne can leave, however, Jaquenetta and Costard appear with the letter that Berowne has written to Rosaline. Although Costard maintains that he received the note from Armado, Berowne quickly discerns what it is and tears it into pieces. Berowne's passion arouses Longaville's suspicions, and while Dumain gathers the pieces of the letter and recognizes Berowne's writing and his name, Berowne confesses to his own violation of their common vow. At Berowne's request Ferdinand dismisses Costard and Jaquenetta.

Following Berowne's defense that love is too strong an emotion for young men to resist and that "Therefore of all hands must we be forsworn," his companions tease him for having fallen in love with Rosaline and exaggerate her dark complexion. Tiring of the quips of his young gallants, the King comments that they are all in love and invites Berowne to show how they may continue their wooing without proving false to their sworn oaths.

In a witty and lengthy piece of casuistry, Berowne reminds the King and his comrades that in their initial oath they were guilty of "flat treason 'gainst the kingly state of youth," and that women's eyes "are the books, the arts, the academes,/That show, contain, and nourish all the world" and are the proper objects of study. Berowne declares that they are even fulfilling their religious duty, "For charity itself fulfils the law." Enthusiastically they "resolve to woo these girls of France" and "win them too."

V,i. The Park

Holofernes, Sir Nathaniel, and Dull are continuing their dinner conversation. While Sir Nathaniel is taking notes on Holofernes's adverse criticism of Don Armado's vocabulary and pronunciation, Armado, Moth, and Costard join them. Holofernes and Don Armado greet each other, and Moth remarks in an aside to Costard, "They have been at a great feast of languages, and stol'n the scraps." In an exchange of affected and high-flown phrases, Armado tells Holofernes that the King has requested him to plan entertainment for the Princess and her company that afternoon and that he wants Holofernes to help him. Immediately Holofernes says that they will portray the Nine Worthies. He declares that Sir Nathaniel will play Joshua, he himself or Don Armado the part of Judas Maccabaeus, Costard that of Pompey the Great, and Moth the role of Hercules. When Don Armado objects that Moth is too small for his part, Holofernes adds that Moth will "present Hercules in minority," and that he will himself play three of the remaining characters. Questioned about his silence, Dull says that he has understood not a word but will gladly participate.

V,ii. The Park

In gay, high spirits over their progress in love, the Princess and her ladies compare the verses and favors they have received from their admirers. Boyet, who has accidentally overheard the King and his companions plotting to disguise themselves as Muscovites when they come to woo their sweethearts, forewarns the maidens. To thwart this scheme the Princess and the other girls resolve to mask themselves, exchange their favors, decline to dance with the gentlemen, and turn their faces away when their lovers address them. The Princess silences Boyet's mild protest with the remark, "There's no such sport as sport by sport o'erthrown."

A trumpet announces the approach of musicians, Moth, and the King and gentlemen disguised as Russians. When Moth garbles his prepared salutation, the ladies turn their backs in pretended scorn. After a preliminary conversation in which Boyet serves as intermediary, the King and his gentlemen, deceived in their identification of the Princess and her attendants, are finally frustrated and withdraw. Pleased with the trick they have played on their suitors, the ladies joke among themselves but wonder what they will do if the gentlemen "return in their own shapes to woo." Rosaline advises that they continue to mock the men and pretend that they did not recognize them in their ridiculous costumes. The Princess and her women retire to their tents as the King and his gentlemen reappear in their proper dress. At the King's request Boyet goes to fetch the Princess, who immediately re-enters with her ladies.

When the King invites the Princess to accompany him to his court, she reminds him that he has previously declined to receive her there because of his vow. He protests that the power of her eye has caused him to violate his oath, but she says that she is most reluctant to be the occasion of the breaking of "heavenly oaths, vow'd with integrity."

After the King apologizes for the barrenness of his hospitality, the Princess replies that she and her ladies have enjoyed their entertainment and that four Russians have recently left them. Thoroughly put down by the Princess and her companions, the King and his gentlemen confess their disguises while the ladies admit their deception in exchanging masks and favors. At this moment, Costard enters to inquire if he and his colleague may produce their play of the Nine Worthies. Berowne and the Princess overcome the King's reservations, and he allows the show to proceed after Armado formally presents a list of characters.

In succession, the amateur actors appear: Costard for Pompey, Sir Nathaniel for Alexander the Great, Holofernes for Judas Maccabaeus, Moth for Hercules, and Armado for Hector. Amidst many interruptions and gibes from their audience, the players attempt to speak their lines. Unexpectedly, Costard steps out of character to charge Don Armado with being responsible for Jaquenetta's pregnancy. Enraged by Costard's accusation and exposure, Don Armado challenges

him. As the two men bluster at each other and contrive excuses for
not beginning the fight, Monsieur Marcade arrives with news that
the King of France, father of the Princess, is dead. The Nine
Worthies withdraw, and the Princess announces her desire to leave
Navarre at once.

In protestations of sincere love, the King and his lords implore the
Princess and her ladies to accept their suits and proposals of marriage.
The Princess answers that she must observe a year of mourning for
her father, but she promises the King that if he will renounce the
pleasures of the world and live in austerity for the same period and
then declare his devotion, she will be his. Each of the Princess's
ladies imposes a similar condition on her suitor and makes the same
promise.

Armado reappears to take his leave and states that as a soldier
and man of honor, he will do justice to Jaquenetta. With the King's
permission he ushers in the cast of the preceding show, and they
sing the "Dialogue of the Owl and the Cuckoo."

A MIDSUMMER NIGHT'S DREAM
[1595–1596]

CHARACTERS

THESEUS, Duke of Athens.

EGEUS, father to *Hermia*.

LYSANDER, ⎱ in love with
DEMETRIUS, ⎰ *Hermia*.

PHILOSTRATE, Master of the
Revels to *Theseus*.

[PETER] QUINCE, a carpenter
(*Prologue*).

SNUG, a joiner (*Lion*).

[NICK] BOTTOM, a weaver
(*Pyramus*).

[FRANCIS] FLUTE, a bellows-
mender (*Thisby*).

[TOM] SNOUT, a tinker (*Wall*).

[ROBIN] STARVELING, a tailor
(*Moonshine*).

HIPPOLYTA, Queen of the Ama-
zons, betrothed to *Theseus*.

HERMIA, daughter to *Egeus*, in
love with *Lysander*.

HELENA, in love with *Demetrius*.

OBERON, King of the Fairies.

TITANIA, Queen of the Fairies.

PUCK, or ROBIN GOODFELLOW.

PEASEBLOSSOM, ⎫
COBWEB, ⎬ fairies.
MOTH, ⎥
MUSTARDSEED, ⎭

Other Fairies attending their
King and Queen. Attendants
on *Theseus* and *Hippolyta*.

Scene: *Athens, and a Nearby Wood*

I,i. Athens. The Palace of Theseus

Theseus and Hippolyta are anticipating their approaching wedding, which they plan to celebrate with the new moon in four days'
time. Theseus orders Philostrate to go into the city and to plan
entertainment for the occasion. At this moment Egeus, with Hermia,
Lysander, and Demetrius, enters with a petition.

Egeus declares that, despite his approval of the marriage of Demetrius and Hermia, Lysander has "bewitch'd the bosom" of his daugh-

38

ter and won her love. Under Athenian law, Egeus claims the privilege of punishing Hermia with death unless she obeys him and marries Demetrius.

Theseus admonishes Hermia that she should yield to her father's judgment, but she stoutly maintains her preference for Lysander, who is as worthy a gentleman as his rival. Courteously, she asks the Duke to indicate the alternatives confronting her if she refuses "to wed Demetrius." Theseus explains that she has two other choices: (1) "to die the death"; (2) "to abjure/For ever the society of men" by assuming the livery of a nun in the service of Diana. He grants her a reprieve until "the next new moon" to make her decision. Demetrius and Lysander begin to argue about their respective merits as suitors, and Lysander accuses Demetrius of having made love to Helena (Nedar's daughter) and then jilting her. Theseus says that he has heard such a rumor and directs Egeus and Demetrius to accompany him and Hippolyta.

Left to themselves, Lysander and Hermia decide to flee Athens and find refuge with Lysander's "widow aunt, a dowager," who lives seven leagues away, beyond the jurisdiction of Athenian law. There they can be married. They agree to meet the following night in the wood, "a league without the town." No sooner have they made these arrangements than Helena joins them. Helena is bemoaning her desertion by Demetrius. When Hermia's insistence that she loves Lysander and despises Demetrius fails to cheer Helena, Hermia reveals the plans of the elopement. After Hermia and Lysander pledge their mutual loyalty and depart, Helena comments on the irrational nature of love and resolves to inform Demetrius of the projected flight of the young couple. She is confident that Demetrius will pursue Hermia, but she may win his thanks for her information. In any event, she will have an excuse to see her former sweetheart.

I,ii. Athens. Quince's House

Quince and his fellows are casting themselves in the interlude they plan to produce in honor of Theseus's wedding. Bottom, eager and irrepressible, wants to play all the parts himself and continually interrupts Quince, who is attempting to interpret the play and its roles to his companions. Finally, Quince assigns Bottom the part of Pyramus, and they all agree to meet the following night "in the palace wood, a mile without the town," where they can "rehearse most obscenely and courageously."

II,i. A Wood near Athens

When a Fairy advises Puck that the Fairy Queen and all her elves are arriving soon, Puck reports Oberon's wrath at Titania's kidnaping of the changeling boy and warns against the Queen's meeting the King in his present mood. In reply to the Fairy's question, Puck admits that he is "that merry wanderer of the night" with many names (Puck, Robin Goodfellow, Hobgoblin) and describes several of his mischievous pranks.

While Puck and the Fairy are conversing, Oberon and Titania arrive with their attendant fairies. The Queen accuses Oberon of having stolen away from fairyland, of having assumed various shapes in order to indulge himself in love affairs, and of enjoying Hippolyta as his mistress. In turn, Oberon charges Titania with being in love with Theseus and with having promoted several of his liaisons. Haughtily, Titania blames Oberon for inciting quarrels, disturbing her pastimes, and precipitating storms in reversal of the seasons. Oberon retorts that Titania may set everything right by returning the changeling boy to him. Titania resolutely declares that she will keep the child, but invites Oberon to join peaceably in their dances until after Theseus's wedding day. The King adamantly demands the boy's return, and Titania and her train depart. Determined to punish Titania, Oberon sends Puck to fetch

> a little Western flower,
> Before milk-white, now purple with love's wound,
> And maidens call it love-in-idleness.

The juice of this flower, the pansy,

> on sleeping eye-lids laid
> Will make or man or woman madly dote
> Upon the next live creature that it sees.

By dropping the concoction in Titania's eyes Oberon will torment her into returning the boy; then he will remove the charm with an antidote. Detecting the approach of Demetrius and Helena, Oberon makes himself invisible in order to "overhear their conference."

Demetrius, exasperated and impatient, is attempting to dissuade the fawning, lovesick Helena from pursuing him. In desperation Demetrius runs away from her, but she persistently follows. Oberon sympathetically comments that Demetrius will seek Helena's love before he leaves the forest. Puck returns with the pansy. Taking the juice with which to streak Titania's eyes, Oberon gives some of it to Puck and orders him to anoint the eyes of a disdainful youth (Demetrius) whom he can recognize "By the Athenian garments he hath on."

II,ii. Another Part of the Wood

After dancing, Titania's fairies sing the Queen to sleep and depart. Oberon appears, squeezes the juice of the flower on Titania's eyelids, and leaves. Now Lysander and Hermia come into view. They have missed their way, and Hermia asks Lysander to find himself a bed while she rests her head "upon this bank." Lysander proposes that "One turf shall serve as pillow for us both," but Hermia circumspectly insists that "in humane modesty" they sleep apart. Lysander agrees to this, and they fall asleep.

Puck, who has searched in vain for an Athenian, discovers Lysander and Hermia. Assuming from Lysander's dress that he is the youth Oberon had in mind, Puck casts the magic juice on his eyes and leaves immediately. At this moment Demetrius runs past, still pursued by Helena. Out of breath, Helena pauses and, seeing Lysander on the ground, wakens him. Instantaneously, Lysander, under the influence of the potion, renounces his attachment for Hermia and declares himself madly in love with Helena. Thinking that Lysander is mocking her, Helena rebukes him and flees. Glancing at Hermia, who is sleeping nearby, Lysander abandons her and goes in pursuit of Helena. Hermia, awakened by a nightmare, calls for Lysander, perceives that she is alone, and almost swoons from fear.

III,i. The Wood. Titania Lying Asleep

Quince, Snug, Bottom, Flute, Snout, and Starveling have assembled to rehearse their interlude of *Pyramus and Thisby*. While they are discussing the problems of production, setting, and stage action, Puck finds them and remains to listen. After Bottom and Flute make ludicrous attempts to con their lines, Puck places an ass's head on Pyramus (i.e., Bottom). Supposing that they "are haunted," Bottom's companions flee. Bottom, innocently unaware of what has happened, thinks that his fellows are trying to scare him. Snout and Quince venture back, tell Bottom that he is "translated," and leave. Still believing that they are attempting "to make an ass" of him and to frighten him, Bottom sings to prove that he is not afraid. His singing wakens the sleeping Titania, who immediately falls in love with the "gentle mortal" with an ass's head. Imploring Bottom to stay with her in the forest, Titania summons Peaseblossom, Cobweb, Moth, and Mustardseed to minister to Bottom and supply his every wish.

III,ii. Another Part of the Wood

Puck reports to Oberon how he has dispersed the "rude mechanicals" and endowed Bottom with an ass's head, and how Titania has fallen in love with the simple weaver. Oberon commends his elfin messenger and asks Puck if he has anointed the Athenian's eyes. Puck asserts that he has, but Demetrius and Hermia appear at this moment, and Puck and Oberon quickly learn that Puck has applied the magic juice to the eyes of the wrong man. Hermia is accusing Demetrius of having slain Lysander in his sleep. Demetrius protests his innocence and his devotion for Hermia, but she orders Demetrius never to see her and departs. Accepting the futility of "following her in this fierce vein," Demetrius lies down to sleep. Oberon, determined to correct the mistake, commands Puck to find Helena of Athens and to bring her where Demetrius will see her when he awakes. In the meantime, Oberon will charm Demetrius's eyes in preparation for Helena's arrival. Oberon sings and applies the magic juice, and Puck returns with news that Helena and Lysander are near at hand. Perceiving that both men will now love Helena, Puck says,

> Shall we their fond pageant see?
> Lord, what fools these mortals be!
> . . . .
> Then will two at once woo one;
> That must needs be sport alone;
> And those things do best please me
> That befall prepost'rously.

While Lysander continues his avowals of love for Helena, Demetrius wakens and vies with Lysander in declaring his love for her. Helena believes that the men have joined in a plot to mock her. Lysander argues that he is willing to yield Hermia to Demetrius, but Demetrius insists that his own infatuation for Hermia is dead. Hermia now approaches; Lysander rebuffs her; and Helena scolds Hermia for collaborating with the two men to make sport of her. With rising bitterness and indignation, the four lovers quarrel until Demetrius and Lysander leave to prove their right to Helena by combat. Hermia and Helena have also come to the point of blows, and they depart separately.

Oberon charges Puck with negligence, but the sprite maintains that his mistake was an honest one. Fearing that Lysander and Demetrius may do violence to each other, Oberon orders Puck to produce a fog and to haunt the two men in such a way as to keep them apart. After they fall asleep from fatigue, Puck is to crush the antidote in Lysander's eyes and thus restore him to his original love of Hermia. While Puck is on this errand, Oberon will find Titania, recover the changeling, and remove the spell whereby the Queen dotes on "the monster." Puck warns of the approach of dawn, when all ghosts and "damned spirits" must hide from the light, but Oberon reminds him that they are spirits of another sort and need not avoid the day. Nevertheless, the King hopes to complete their business before morning breaks.

While Lysander and Demetrius pass back and forth in search of each other, Puck misleads and confuses them until both lie down in exhaustion and fall asleep. Soon, Helena and Hermia, tired from wandering in the forest, appear and go to sleep near the two men. Singing, Puck squeezes the corrective juice on Lysander's eyes, and concludes:

> That every man should take his own,
> In your waking shall be shown.
> > Jack shall have Jill;
> > Nought shall go ill;
> The man shall have his mare again, and all shall be well.

IV,i. The Wood. (The Four Lovers Lying Asleep)

Titania continues her coddling of Bottom while he incongruously basks in the attention of the fairy attendants. At last Bottom has "an exposition of sleep come" upon him and dozes in Titania's arms. She dismisses the fairies, dotes on her misshapen lover, and also goes to sleep. Oberon, who has been observing all that has happened, advances and describes to Puck the absurdities of the night. Having upbraided Titania for her doting and induced her to return the changeling boy, Oberon begins to pity his Queen and orders Puck to remove the ass's head from Bottom after the King restores Titania from her spell. On waking, Titania thinks that she has had a bad dream and loathes the sight of Bottom. Puck takes off the ass's head, and Oberon and Titania dance and sing to celebrate their reconciliation.

As the Fairies leave, Theseus, Hippolyta, Egeus, and attendants appear on their early morning fox hunt. They find the sleeping lovers, and Theseus, recalling that this is the day on which Hermia must state her decision, orders his huntsmen to waken the sleepers with their horns. In reply to the Duke's question, Lysander, who is only half awake, admits that he and Hermia were fleeing Athens. Egeus interrupts to demand that Theseus pronounce the full penalty of the law on Lysander.

Before Theseus can respond, Demetrius tells how he pursued the elopers but now finds that he has lost his love for Hermia and wishes to woo Helena, to whom he was formerly betrothed. Overruling Egeus, Theseus suggests that all return to Athens, where they will celebrate a threefold marriage. Confused but happy, Demetrius, Lysander, Hermia, and Helena agree that they have experienced strange dreams and follow the royal party. Bottom, last to awake from the magic spell, thinks that he is still at the rehearsal of the interlude, remembers "a most rare vision," but decides that he will be an ass if he attempts to expound it. He may induce Peter Quince to write a ballad about it and call it "Bottom's Dream."

IV,ii. Athens. Quince's House

Quince, Flute, Snout, and Starveling are much concerned over Bottom's absence, for they cannot find anyone else to play the part of Pyramus. Snug comes in with the news that there have been multiple weddings in the temple, and he speculates that they would have earned rich rewards if they could have produced the interlude. While they lament their bad luck, Bottom appears, declines to tell his fellows what has happened, and exhorts them to hasten their preparations for the play.

V,i. Athens. The Palace of Theseus

Hippolyta and Theseus are discussing the remarkable experiences of the young lovers in the wood, and Theseus expatiates on the imagination of "The lunatic, the lover, and the poet." When the two couples enter, Theseus asks Philostrate what masques, dances, and "revels are in hand" to "wear away this long age of three hours/ Between our after-supper and bed-time." Philostrate presents a list of "how many sports are ripe," and the Duke finds special interest in

> 'A tedious brief scene of young Pyramus
> And his love Thisby: very tragical mirth.'

Philostrate describes the play as an unworthy amateur production, but when Theseus learns that "Hard-handed men that work in Athens" have prepared it in celebration of the royal wedding, he determines to hear it in spite of Philostrate's and Hippolyta's objections.

Forthwith Philostrate presents Quince, who acts as Prologue to the interlude. In their sincere and bungling fashion "the mechanicals" present their play while members of the audience joke about the actors' enthusiastic ineptitude. Finally, after Bottom steps out of character to converse with the Duke and Starveling forgets his lines as Moonshine and improvises, the interlude ends with Pyramus's death and Thisby's suicide. Thanking the artisans and commending them for their efforts, Theseus declines "to see the Epilogue" but consents "to hear a Bergomask dance" between two of the company. After the performance of the dance, Theseus proclaims a fortnight of revels and jollity as all depart for their respective wedding beds.

Puck enters and sweeps the house with a broom since it is the time of night when fairies are frolicsome. Oberon and Titania appear with their elfin attendants. Singing and dancing, they invoke a blessing on the house, on the three marriages, and on all future issue. They leave Puck to seek the plaudits of the audience, who, if the actors have given offense, may consider the incidents they have witnessed to be a dream.

THE MERCHANT OF VENICE [1596–1597]

CHARACTERS

THE DUKE OF VENICE.

THE PRINCE OF
  MOROCCO,
THE PRINCE OF } suitors to *Portia.*
  ARRAGON,

ANTONIO, a Merchant of Venice.

BASSANIO, his friend, suitor to *Portia.*

SOLANIO,[1]
SALERIO,
[SALARINO.] [2] } friends to *Antonio* and *Bassanio.*
GRATIANO,

LORENZO, in love with *Jessica.*

SHYLOCK, a rich Jew.

TUBAL, a Jew, his friend.

LAUNCELOT GOBBO, a clown, servant to *Shylock.*

OLD GOBBO, father to *Launcelot.*

LEONARDO, servant to *Bassanio.*

BALTHASAR,
STEPHANO, } servants to *Portia.*

PORTIA [BALTHAZAR],[3] an heiress.

NERISSA, her waiting-maid.

JESSICA, daughter to *Shylock.*

Magnificoes of Venice, Officers of the Court of Justice, Jailor, Servants, and other Attendants.

Scene: *Venice; Portia's House at Belmont*

I,i. Venice. A Street

Salerio and Solanio are convinced that Antonio's sadness and melancholy spring from his concern over trading vessels presently at sea. He assures them, however, that he has diversified investments

---

[1] Some editors prefer to spell this name "Salanio."

[2] Many editors omit Salarino from the list of characters. Other editors substitute Salarino for Salerio in I,i; II,iv,vi, and viii; and in III,i. Several designate Salarino for Solanio in III,iii. In V,i, some ascribe lines 15 and 107–109 to Solanio; others give the same lines to Salerio.

[3] Some editors prefer to spell Portia's assumed name like that of her servant, "Balthasar."

and that he is not worried about his fortune. They accuse him of being in love, but he makes light of this suggestion. Salerio and Solanio leave upon the arrival of Bassanio, Lorenzo, and Gratiano.

After exchanging views on melancholy and gaiety, Gratiano and Lorenzo agree to meet Antonio and Bassanio for dinner and depart. Bassanio comments on Gratiano's garrulity and then tells Antonio of the numerous debts he has incurred and the impoverishment of his estate. On Antonio's promise to help in any way he can, Bassanio reveals his plan of wooing Portia, the beautiful and wealthy heiress of Belmont. Requiring additional capital to make a favorable impression among his many rival suitors, Bassanio asks Antonio for one more loan. Antonio reminds Bassanio that he has reinvested all of his money in his maritime ventures, but he generously empowers his friend to ascertain what sums he can borrow on Antonio's credit in Venice.

I,ii. Belmont. Portia's House

Portia and Nerissa are chatting about the terms of Portia's inheritance. Portia finds herself uncomfortably restricted by the clause in her father's will which directs that she marry the suitor who correctly selects the secretly designated one of three caskets: gold, silver, and lead. Nerissa defends the inspiration of Portia's deceased father and asks Portia if she has affection for any of her present suitors.

Wittily and disparagingly, Portia describes: the Neapolitan prince ("a colt indeed"); the County Palatine ("He doth nothing but frown"); the French lord, Monsieur Le Bon ("God made him, and therefore let him pass for a man"); Falconbridge, a young English baron ("How oddly he is suited"); a Scottish lord ("he borrowed a box of the ear of the Englishman, and swore he would pay him again when he was able"); and a young German, nephew of the Duke of Savoy ("When he is best, he is little worse than a man"). Nerissa tells her mistress that all of these have refused to submit to the test of choosing the right casket, and Portia welcomes this excuse to rid herself of them and says she is determined to follow her father's instructions.

Nerissa asks Portia if she remembers a Venetian, "a scholar and a soldier," who visited Belmont in her father's lifetime. Portia recalls Bassanio and seconds Nerissa's praise of him. A servant enters to announce the departure of various suitors and the arrival of another, the Prince of Morocco, on the morrow.

I,iii. Venice. A Public Place

Shylock, carefully analyzing Antonio's security, decides that the Merchant's credit rating is good and tells Bassanio that he will accept Antonio's bond for three thousand ducats for three months. He wishes to speak with Antonio but declines Bassanio's invitation to dinner, saying that he will do business with Christians but will not meet them socially.

At this instant Antonio approaches, and, in an aside, Shylock voices his hatred for Antonio because he is a Christian, because he undermines Shylock's banking ventures by lending money without interest, because he dislikes Jews, and because he publicly condemns Shylock and his financial practices. Shylock also privately reflects that he will have to borrow from his fellow Hebrew, Tubal, in order to raise three thousand ducats in cash.

Somewhat haughtily, Antonio informs Shylock that, to accommodate his friend Bassanio, he will violate his custom of neither lending nor borrowing at interest. Shylock lectures Antonio on the propriety of charging interest, using illustrations from Old Testament history. Becoming impatient, Antonio asks Shylock if he intends to lend the money. Unwilling to be rushed, Shylock recalls many insults he has suffered at Antonio's hands and inquires if "for these courtesies" he expects Shylock to do him a favor. Repudiating any suggestion of establishing a friendship, Antonio tells Shylock that he should lend the money as if to an enemy and exact the full penalty if the debtor does not fulfill the conditions of the loan.

Saying that he wishes to "be friends with you and have your love," Shylock informs Antonio that he will forget past insults and supply the money with no interest charges at all. Instead, he suggests that "in a merry sport" Antonio pledge a pound of his flesh from whatever part of his body Shylock chooses to cut it, if he fails to repay the loan by the specified date. Antonio cheerfully and confidently agrees to go with Shylock to a notary's and sign the bond, although Bassanio likes "not fair terms and a villain's mind."

II,i. Portia's House

In the presence of their attendants, the Prince of Morocco boasts to Portia of his conquests on the fields of arms and love and asks her to lead him to the caskets in order that he may submit to the test for her hand. Reminding him that he must swear "Never to speak to lady afterward/In way of marriage" if he chooses the wrong one, Portia tells him that he may try his fortune after dinner.

II,ii. Venice. A Street

In a humorous monologue, Launcelot Gobbo debates whether he should listen to the fiend, who prompts him to run away from Shylock, or obey his conscience, which tells him to remain in the Jew's service. Just as he decides that he will run away, his father, Old Gobbo, approaches with a basket, inquires "the way to Master Jew's," and asks if "one Launcelot . . . dwell with him or no." Old Gobbo is almost blind and cannot believe that the Clown is really his son. At last convinced, he tells Launcelot that he is bringing Shylock a present, but Launcelot urges his father to make the gift to Bassanio, into whose employment Launcelot wishes to transfer.

Offering the doves in the basket to Bassanio, who has just appeared, Old Gobbo adds his voice to Launcelot's in requesting that the Clown become a member of Bassanio's retinue. Bassanio employs Launcelot, sends him to take his leave of Shylock, and orders a servant to prepare a special livery for his new retainer. Bassanio sends Leonardo on an errand, and Gratiano enters with the special request that Bassanio take him along to Belmont. Bassanio consents on condition that Gratiano allay his "skipping spirit" "with some cold drops of modesty."

II,iii. Venice. Shylock's House

Jessica, sad at Launcelot's departure, rewards the Clown and asks him to deliver a letter to Lorenzo. Launcelot leaves lest Shylock find them talking together, and Jessica confesses her shame in being Shylock's child and her resolution to profess Christianity and marry Lorenzo.

II,iv. Venice. A Street

On his way to invite Shylock to sup with Bassanio, Launcelot delivers Jessica's letter to Lorenzo, who with Gratiano, Salerio, and Solanio, is making preparations for a masque at dinner that evening. Lorenzo tips Launcelot and sends a message to Jessica that he will not fail her. Alone with Gratiano, Lorenzo tells his friend that he plans to elope with Jessica, who will supply herself with gold and jewels, disguise herself as a page, and act as his torchbearer in the masque.

II,v. Venice. In Front of Shylock's House

Launcelot meets Shylock, who instructs Jessica in how she is to protect his house and property while he is dining with Bassanio. When Launcelot intimates that there will be masques, Shylock particularly cautions Jessica against gazing "on Christian fools with varnish'd faces." Launcelot manages to convey Lorenzo's message in a parting jingle. Shylock comments that Launcelot is a kind enough fool but has a huge appetite and will "help to waste" Bassanio's "borrowed purse." Left to herself, Jessica discloses that she will leave home before Shylock returns.

II,vi. Venice. In Front of Shylock's House

Gratiano and Salerio, costumed as masquers, appear and wait for Lorenzo, who shortly comes and calls for Jessica. Throwing down a casket, Jessica apologizes for her masculine attire, acquires more money, and joins them. Lorenzo, Jessica, and Salerio leave to present the masque at Bassanio's feast. Antonio meets Gratiano and informs him that Bassanio, not waiting for the masque, is ready to sail as soon as Gratiano comes aboard.

II,vii. Belmont. Portia's House

Portia conducts the Prince of Morocco to the three caskets and tells him that if he chooses the one containing her picture he will win her for his wife. After reading the inscriptions and ruminating on them, the Prince selects the golden one and opens it. He finds "A carrion Death, within whose empty eye/There is a written scroll." Morocco reads the poem, which begins with the line "All that glisters is not gold," and hurriedly departs. Portia hopes that "all of his complexion" may have similar success in wooing her.

II,viii. Venice. A Street

Salerio and Solanio are chatting about the futile efforts of Shylock to detain Bassanio's ship in the belief that Jessica and Lorenzo were aboard. They agree that Shylock, outraged by Jessica's elopement with a Christian and by the loss of his money and jewels and by the mocking of the boys in Venice, is now likely to exact his revenge on Antonio should the Christian merchant fail to pay his debt. Salerio has heard news of the shipwreck of a Venetian vessel in the English Channel, and he hopes that it was not one of Antonio's. Praising

Antonio's kindness and generosity, they start to "find him out/And quicken his embraced heaviness/With some delight or other."

II,ix. Belmont. Portia's House

Ready to make his selection of the three caskets, the Prince of Arragon repeats his vows: (1) never to reveal which casket he chooses; (2) if he selects the wrong one, never to propose marriage to any maid; (3) and if he fails to win Portia, to leave immediately. After studying the respective inscriptions and weighing them in his mind, Arragon chooses the silver casket. He finds the portrait of a blinking idiot, reads the attached poem, and leaves. A messenger announces the arrival of another suitor, a young Venetian, and Nerissa hopes that it is Bassanio.

III,i. Venice. A Street

While Solanio and Salerio discuss the persistent report that one of Antonio's ships has wrecked on the Goodwin Sands, Shylock appears and accuses them of knowing about Jessica's elopement. In reply to their questions, Shylock declares that Antonio is now bankrupt, has lost his credit rating, and would do well to look to his bond. Salerio suggests that Shylock will not actually take Antonio's flesh in forfeit, but Shylock excitedly retorts that if a Jew takes his revenge against a Christian he is merely following Christian example. A servant summons Solanio and Salerio to Antonio's house.

Tubal, a Jewish friend of Shylock, has been searching for Jessica but has been unable to find her. In Genoa, however, he heard that Antonio had lost another vessel. This news elates Shylock, but Tubal distresses him just as quickly by telling him that Jessica spent eighty ducats in one night. Gladdened by the report of Antonio's financial reverses and enraged that Jessica traded a valuable turquoise ring for a monkey, Shylock sends Tubal to have an officer ready to arrest Antonio if he cannot redeem the loan.

III,ii. Belmont. Portia's House

In love with Bassanio and enjoying his company, Portia pleads with him to delay making his selection of the casket. Although she could tell him which one to choose, she is unwilling to forswear herself, and she is fearful lest he designate the wrong one and have to leave her. Bassanio will live in torture, however, until he learns the outcome, and he insists on risking his fate at once. Instructing Nerissa and the other attendants to stand aside, Portia orders music and a song and prepares to view Bassanio's selection "with much much more dismay" than he himself senses. The song

> Tell me, where is fancy bred,
> Or in the heart, or in the head? [1]

provides an accompaniment "the whilst Bassanio comments on the caskets to himself." Remembering that outward shows mean little and that plainness is more moving than eloquence, he chooses the leaden casket. Opening it, he finds Portia's portrait and a scroll instructing him to claim her with a kiss. Overjoyed, Bassanio hesitates to accept his success until Portia herself confirms it. Modestly disclaiming her manifest charms and talents, Portia commits herself, her property, and her household to Bassanio. To seal the pledge, she gives him a ring which he vows to keep on his finger as long as he lives.

At this point, Nerissa and Gratiano seek permission to celebrate their own marriage when Portia and Bassanio celebrate theirs. In the midst of the gaiety, Lorenzo, Jessica, and Salerio arrive from Venice. Lorenzo apologizes for coming to Belmont but says that Salerio persuaded him to do so. Salerio gives Bassanio a letter from Antonio. Bassanio pales as he reads of the loss of all Antonio's ships; Salerio describes Shylock's relentless determination to exact the forfeit; and Jessica testifies that she has heard her father swear that he would rather have Antonio's flesh than twenty times the principal of the debt. With some embarrassment, Bassanio has confessed his impoverished state to Portia, and he now tells her that Antonio owes Shylock three thousand ducats for his sake. Portia says that as soon as she and Bassanio are married, he must go to Venice, redeem the bond at any cost, and return with Antonio to Belmont.

III,iii. Venice. A Street in Front of Shylock's House

Shylock, set on revenge, turns a deaf ear to Antonio, who, under custody of the Jailor, has come to discuss his situation with the Jew. Shylock rebukes the Jailor for bringing Antonio to him and leaves. Solanio believes that the Duke will set aside the penalty, but Antonio accepts the fact that the Duke must enforce laws literally in order to protect the reputation of Venice as a world market. He hopes that Bassanio will arrive before he has to pay the forfeit.

---

[1] A few critics have suggested that this song affords Bassanio a helpful clue in arriving at the correct decision; the majority insist that it does not.

III,iv. Belmont. Portia's House

Portia tells Lorenzo that she and Nerissa will await their husbands' return in a monastery two miles distant. She asks him to manage her household in her absence, and he and Jessica withdraw. Immediately Portia calls Balthasar and sends him to her cousin, Doctor Bellario, in Padua, with a request for certain notes and clothes which Balthasar is to bring her on the way to Venice. While they prepare for their journey, Portia tells Nerissa that they will both assume the guise of young men.

III,v. Belmont. Near Portia's House

Launcelot is jesting with Jessica about her non-Christian ancestry. Lorenzo joins them and turns the tables on the Clown by accusing him of immorality with a Moorish woman. Launcelot leaves with instructions for the other servants, and Jessica and Lorenzo praise Portia's exceptional beauty and talents.

IV,i. Venice. A Court of Justice

Before the Duke and Magnificoes of Venice, Antonio and his friends prepare to answer Shylock's suit. The Duke voices pity for Antonio but says that no argument has moved the Jew to relent. Antonio quietly replies that he is ready to suffer "The very tyranny and rage" of Shylock's spirit.

Commanding Shylock to appear in court, the Duke appeals to the moneylender to show pity on Antonio's losses by releasing the merchant from the forfeiture and by reducing the amount of the principal. Shylock declares that he has sworn a holy vow to exact the penalty, that it is his "humour" to do so, and that he can give no reason other "than a lodg'd hate and a certain loathing" for Antonio. Bassanio attempts to argue with Shylock, but Antonio advises his friend that such pleading is futile. Bassanio offers Shylock six thousand ducats in payment of the debt, but Shylock contemptuously refuses to accept this settlement. The Duke inquires how Shylock can hope for mercy when he renders none, but the Jew insists that he has done no wrong, that he has paid dearly for the pound of flesh, and that he "will have it."

At this point, the Duke threatens to dismiss court unless Bellario, a learned lawyer, comes to assist in the case. Solanio announces the arrival of a messenger bringing letters from Bellario in Padua. The messenger, who is Nerissa dressed like a lawyer's clerk, presents a letter to the Duke. While Shylock whets his knife, the Duke glances at the communication and details three or four attendants to usher in the young and learned Doctor Balthazar, whom Bellario has delegated to state his legal opinions. Portia, impersonating Balthazar, enters.

With the Duke's permission, Portia takes over the conduct of the case. Antonio confesses the bond, and Portia delivers an eloquent plea to Shylock to show mercy. Portia inquires if Antonio can pay the money, whereupon Bassanio offers three times the principal. Shylock remains adamant, and Portia declares that "no power in Venice/ Can alter a decree established." Praising the wisdom of the young judge, Shylock refuses to relent. Portia commands Antonio to bare his bosom and tells Shylock, who has balances to weigh the flesh, to proceed. Portia inquires if Shylock also has a surgeon in readiness to minister to Antonio, but the Jew argues that the bond did not specify this service. Antonio, Bassanio, and Gratiano exchange farewells, and Shylock prepares to collect his forfeit.

Suddenly, Portia interrupts to remind Shylock that although the law of Venice awards him the pound of flesh, it also specifies that if he sheds one drop of Christian blood he must surrender all his land and goods to the state. Swiftly reversing his position, Shylock says that he will accept three times the amount of the debt and release Antonio. Bassanio starts to pay the sum, but Portia intervenes and declares that Shylock will have absolute justice and must take the stipulated forfeit. She also decrees that if Shylock miscalculates the weight of the flesh by the smallest fraction he will be executed. While Gratiano taunts the usurer, Portia tells Shylock that he cannot recover his principal but must take the forfeiture at his own peril.

Shylock turns to leave, but Portia further directs that inasmuch as he, an alien, has plotted against the life of a Venetian citizen, he must pay half his goods to his intended victim and the other half to the state. In addition, his life itself lies within the Duke's discretion.

In a display of Christian mercy, the Duke grants Shylock his life and suggests that humbleness may reduce the state's half of the penalty to a fine. Frantically, Shylock urges that the Duke sentence him to death rather than take his property. Antonio, in turn, shows even greater generosity and mercy on condition: (1) that Shylock assign Antonio half of his estate to invest for Lorenzo; (2) that Shylock immediately embrace Christianity; and (3) that he bequeath all of his estate to Lorenzo and Jessica. Shylock accepts these terms and leaves.

Bassanio, overwhelmed with gratitude, offers Portia (in the person of Balthazar) the three thousand ducats for her services, but she disclaims mercenary motives, accounts the satisfaction of having saved Antonio ample reward, and hopes that Bassanio will know her when they meet again. Upon his insistence that she accept "some remembrance," Portia says that she will wear his gloves and take the ring she sees on his hand. Bassanio refuses to surrender the ring because of the vow he has sworn to his wife. Chiding and taunting him, Portia says that the ring is all she really wants and that his wife would approve his giving it to her, and she leaves. Antonio urges Bassanio to risk his wife's displeasure by yielding the ring to the young lawyer, and Bassanio sends Gratiano to give it to Portia.

IV,ii. Venice. A Street

Still disguised, Portia is arranging with Nerissa to get Shylock's signature on the deed, which they will take to Lorenzo. Gratiano finds them, gives Portia the ring, and invites them to dinner. Portia accepts the ring, declines the dinner, and asks Gratiano to conduct Nerissa to Shylock's house. Nerissa mischievously determines to get Gratiano's ring from him.

V,i. Belmont. In Front of Portia's House

Lorenzo and Jessica are tenderly trading endearments when Stephano interrupts with the news that Portia and Nerissa will arrive before daybreak. No sooner has Stephano completed his announcement than Launcelot appears with word that Bassanio will also return before morning. Lorenzo suggests to Jessica that they await the travelers outside and sends Stephano to provide music for the homecoming of master and mistress.

Portia and Nerissa appear, cheered by the light in the house and by the music. They see Lorenzo and Jessica in the moonlight. On satisfying herself that Bassiano and Gratiano have not preceded her and Nerissa, Portia commands that no one reveal her and Nerissa's absence from Belmont.

Portia cordially welcomes Bassanio and Antonio. Meanwhile Nerissa has cornered Gratiano and accused him of giving his ring to some woman; she refuses to believe that he gave it to "a little scrubbed boy, . . . the judge's clerk." Overhearing the quarrel, Portia reprimands Gratiano and says that she is sure that Bassanio would never have parted with the ring she gave him. Defending himself, Gratiano reveals that Bassanio also gave his ring away. Pretending great indignation and disappointment, Portia says that she will not come in Bassanio's bed until she sees the ring. She also warns that unless Bassanio remains with her constantly she will have the young lawyer for her bedfellow. To Gratiano's confusion and frustration, Nerissa echoes her mistress's threats.

Protesting that he is the cause of all the misunderstanding, Antonio beseeches Portia to forgive Bassanio and vows to stand surety for his friend. Portia hands Antonio a ring and says, "Give him this,/ And bid him keep it better than the other." Bassanio recognizes the ring as the one Portia first gave him.

Taunting her husband further, Portia declares that the young lawyer lay with her, and Nerissa confesses that she slept the night before with the lawyer's clerk. Gratiano grumbles that he and Bassanio have been cuckolded, but Portia produces a letter from Bellario in which he identifies Doctor Balthazar and his assistant. Portia also gives Antonio the welcome news that three of his merchantmen have safely arrived in port. Lorenzo and Jessica learn that they are to inherit Shylock's wealth, and all go to the house to celebrate their good fortunes.

MUCH ADO ABOUT NOTHING
[1598–1599]

CHARACTERS

DON PEDRO, Prince of Arragon.

DON JOHN, his bastard brother.

CLAUDIO, a young lord of Florence.

BENEDICK, a young lord of Padua.

LEONATO, Governor of Messina.

ANTONIO, an old man, his brother.

BALTHASAR, attendant on *Don Pedro*.

BORACHIO,⎫ followers of *Don*
CONRADE, ⎭ *John*.

FRIAR FRANCIS.

DOGBERRY, a constable.

VERGES, a headborough.

A Sexton [*Francis Seacoal*].

A Boy.

[*Antonio's* Son.]

HERO, daughter to *Leonato*.

BEATRICE, niece to *Leonato*.

MARGARET,⎫ gentlewoman
URSULA, ⎬ attending
⎭ on *Hero*.

Messengers, Watch [*Hugh Oatcake, George Seacoal*], Attendants.

Scene: *Messina*

I,i. In Front of Leonato's House

A messenger brings Leonato a letter announcing the imminent arrival of Don Pedro. The messenger also reports the gallantry of Claudio in Don Pedro's recent victory. Beatrice asks for news of Benedick, and the messenger replies that the young Paduan is returning unharmed. While Beatrice makes caustic remarks about Benedick, Leonato explains that his niece and Benedick never meet "but there's a skirmish of wit between them."

When Don Pedro and his retinue arrive, Benedick and Beatrice engage in a characteristic battle of wits. Don Pedro interrupts to tell his companions that Leonato has invited the entire company to enjoy his hospitality. When Leonato extends his welcome to Don John, the bastard brother is barely polite in his reply. Privately Claudio questions Benedick about Hero and admits that he has lost his heart to her at first sight. Don Pedro returns and orders Benedick to explain his and Claudio's lagging behind. Benedick tells him that Claudio has fallen in love with Hero. Don Pedro praises Hero and approves the match. All the while, Benedick proclaims his cynical distaste for women and boasts that he will continue to live as a bachelor. Benedick leaves to convey Don Pedro's regards to Leonato. On hearing Claudio's avowal of love for Hero, Don Pedro volunteers to promote his friend's suit by impersonating Claudio to gain Hero's attention and favor. Don Pedro will then divulge the truth to Leonato and win his consent to the marriage.

I,ii. Leonato's House

Leonato is talking with his old brother, Antonio, about entertainment of the guests. Antonio, basing his information on a report by one of his servants who has overheard and misunderstood the conversation between Don Pedro and Claudio, tells Leonato that Don Pedro plans to propose marriage to Hero. Hesitant to accept the news at face value, Leonato nevertheless starts to forewarn and prepare his daughter. Antonio's Son enters with a Musician and other attendants, and Leonato gives them further instructions.

I,iii. Leonato's House

In another room Don John, conversing with Conrade, confesses himself to be a chronically melancholic man, averse to currying favor with Don Pedro, and possessing a surly disposition. "It must not be denied," he says, "but I am a plain-dealing villain." Borachio, who has heard Don Pedro and Claudio discussing their plan to win Hero for Claudio, enters and reveals the scheme to Don John. Instantly Don John sees an opportunity to thwart Claudio, for whom he has an envious hatred.

II,i. Leonato's House

Leonato and Antonio are discussing the absence from supper of Don John. After Beatrice and Hero comment on Don John's tartness and melancholy, the conversation turns to Benedick, whom Beatrice insists she also finds unattractive. She adds that she scorns all men and will not marry until God makes men "of some other metal than earth." Leonato reminds Hero of Don Pedro's anticipated proposal, and Beatrice gives her cousin some jocular advice on courting. Antonio leaves and, masking himself, immediately returns with the guests, who are also wearing visors.

Chatting together, Don Pedro and Hero move aside, as do Balthasar and Margaret. Pretending that she does not recognize Benedick, with whom she is talking, Beatrice characterizes him as "the Prince's jester, a very dull fool." The maskers move to another room, leaving Don John, Borachio, and Claudio together.

Correctly identifying Claudio, Don John pretends to think that he is Benedick and urges him to dissuade Don Pedro from wooing Hero because she is not of suitable rank. As Don John and Borachio go to the banquet, Claudio mistakenly concludes that Don Pedro has proved false and is courting Hero for himself. At this moment Benedick comes back and strengthens Claudio's suspicions by telling him that Don Pedro has won Hero. Claudio leaves, and Benedick declares that he will plan appropriate punishment on Beatrice for her raillery.

Don Pedro returns to reassure Benedick that he is promoting Claudio's suit with Hero rather than interfering with it. Their conversation turns to Beatrice, and Benedick repeats his dislike for her and says that he "would not marry her, though she were endowed with all that Adam had left him before he transgress'd." As Claudio, Beatrice, Leonato, and Hero approach, Benedick implores Don Pedro to send him on any errand so long as it takes him away from Beatrice. Benedick leaves, and Don Pedro tells Beatrice that she has "lost the heart of Signior Benedick."

Observing Claudio's sad appearance, Don Pedro informs his young follower that he has wooed Hero in Claudio's name and obtained Leonato's consent. He tells Claudio to name the day of the marriage. In the midst of the rejoicing, Beatrice good-naturedly comments on her own failure to find a husband and leaves. Don Pedro suggests that she would prove an excellent wife for Benedick, but Leonato says "if they were but a week married, they would talk themselves mad." Although Claudio wishes to celebrate his wedding the following day, Leonato insists that the couple postpone the date a week in order to make suitable preparations. Don Pedro enlists the willing help of Claudio, Hero, and Leonato in promoting a match between Benedick and Beatrice.

II,ii. Leonato's House

Borachio and Don John are plotting to prevent the marriage of Claudio and Hero. Borachio, who has won and enjoyed the favors of Margaret, will arrange a clandestine meeting with his mistress, who will impersonate Hero. He will stage this scene on the eve of the proposed marriage, at the same time finding a pretext to lure Hero away while Don John conducts Don Pedro and Claudio to witness Hero's supposed perfidy. Don John promises Borachio one thousand ducats if he succeeds.

II,iii. Leonato's Orchard

Benedick sends a boy to fetch him a book; then he soliloquizes on Claudio's desertion of military life for the pleasures and pains of wooing. Benedick fancies himself immune to the charms of any woman. Seeing his friends approaching, Benedick hides in the arbor.

While Balthasar provides music, Don Pedro, Claudio, and Leonato prepare to bait the eavesdropping Benedick. Dismissing Balthasar and his musicians, they discuss Beatrice's growing love for Benedick and her resolution not to divulge her affection to him. They express pity for Beatrice, but they hesitate to inform Benedick lest he "torment the poor lady worse." Pretending to view the situation as hopeless, the schemers stroll out of Benedick's earreach and plan to spread "the same net" for Beatrice.

Completely deceived by the conversation he has overheard, Benedick reflects on Beatrice's charms and virtues, recants his resolution not to wed, and says, "When I said I would die a bachelor, I did not think I should live till I were married." When Beatrice comes to call him to dinner, Benedick spies "some marks of love in her" and decides that he is a villain if he does not return her affection.

III,i. Leonato's Orchard

Hero dispatches Margaret to fetch Beatrice to overhear a conversation with Ursula designed to convince Beatrice of Benedick's lovesickness for her. After Beatrice conceals herself in the arbor, Hero and Ursula agree that Beatrice's self-love and disdain make it useless for anyone to inform her of Benedick's true regard for her. When Hero and Ursula leave to review Hero's wardrobe, Beatrice emerges from hiding. Now convinced of Benedick's love for her and blaming herself for her former pride and scorn, she resolves to welcome his wooing.

III,ii. Leonato's House

In a merry mood before Claudio's wedding, Don Pedro, Claudio, and Leonato remark on Benedick's changed manner. After Benedick draws Leonato aside for a private conference, Don John enters and, having learned that Claudio will be married on the morrow, abruptly declares Hero to be disloyal. Shocked by the news, Don Pedro and Claudio consent to watch with Don John outside Hero's window. If proof of Don John's accusation is forthcoming, they will denounce and disgrace her in church the following day.

III,iii. A Street

Dogberry and Verges are posting watchmen and giving them instructions. In his homespun and blundering manner, Dogberry cautions his men to be particularly vigilant in the vicinity of Leonato's house. When Dogberry and Verges leave, Borachio and Conrade appear. Borachio is telling Conrade how he has earned a thousand ducats by impersonating Hero's lover with Margaret, who took the part of Hero. Having overheard Borachio's account, the two watchmen place Borachio and Conrade under arrest and march them off for interrogation.

III,iv. Leonato's House

Hero sends Ursula for Beatrice while Margaret assists her mistress in selecting her trousseau. Beatrice joins them, and they gossip gaily until Ursula reappears with word that Claudio and his groomsmen have come to escort Hero to church.

III,v. Leonato's House

In their rambling and loquacious manner, Dogberry and Verges inform Leonato that they have two "arrant knaves," "aspicious persons," under arrest. In haste to get to his daughter's wedding, Leonato tells them to conduct the interrogation themselves and hurries off with the messenger who comes for him. Dogberry, determined to prove as efficient as possible, sends Verges to fetch Francis Seacoal, the Sexton, to take down a written record of the hearing.

IV,i. A Church

Leonato urges Friar Francis to conduct a brief marriage ceremony, but the Friar inquires if anyone present knows of "any inward impediment" to the match. Denouncing Hero as a "rotten orange" and impugning her chastity, Claudio declares that he will not marry her. To the astonishment of Hero and Leonato, Claudio persists in his accusations, with the support of Don Pedro and Don John. When Hero denies having conversed with a man at her window on the preceding night, Don Pedro swears on his honor that he, Don John, and Claudio saw and heard her do so. Hero swoons; Leonato wishes that some friend would end his life by killing him; Don Pedro, Don John, and Claudio stalk out.

While Beatrice and Friar Francis try to revive Hero, Leonato laments his daughter's loss of honor. Restored to consciousness, Hero persists in affirming her innocence, as Beatrice, Benedick, and the Friar defend her reputation to her father. Trusting in the integrity of Don Pedro and Claudio, Benedick attributes the misunderstanding to "John the bastard,/Whose spirits toil in frame of villainies." Beside himself, Leonato vows to tear Hero to pieces if she proves guilty or to avenge himself on those who have wronged her if she establishes her innocence.

Seeking some solution, Friar Francis advises Leonato to proclaim that Hero has died from the shock of Claudio's denunciation. Grief for her may abate suspicions; otherwise she may withdraw from active society in "some reclusive and religious life." When Benedick supports the plan, Leonato agrees. Left to themselves, Benedick and Beatrice acknowledge their love for each other. When Beatrice asks Benedick to prove his love by killing Claudio for his insult to her cousin, Benedick demurs but in the face of her indignation consents to challenge his friend.

IV,ii. A Prison

Dogberry, Verges, and the Sexton arrive in robes to conduct the examination of Conrade and Borachio, who enter under guard. In bungling fashion, the watchmen testify to the slandering of Hero. Having heard of the flight of Don John, the accusation of Hero in church, and her reported death, the Sexton recognizes the importance of the inquiry and instructs Dogberry to take the prisoners to Leonato. Dogberry complies, although he regards the fact that Conrade has called him an ass as the worst of the legal offenses.

V,i. A Street near Leonato's House

Leonato, breathing out violence against the dishonorers of his daughter, turns a deaf ear to Antonio's counsel of patience. When

Don Pedro and Claudio appear, Leonato charges Claudio with having falsely accused Hero and thus causing her death. Antonio adds his voice to that of Leonato, but Don Pedro and Claudio are eager to avoid further controversy with the outraged father and uncle. Vowing that they will have satisfaction, Leonato and Antonio leave as Benedick enters.

Unsuccessfully, Benedick attempts to goad Claudio into fighting with him. Claudio cannot see any reason for Benedick's challenge, and Don Pedro thinks that Benedick is jesting. Frustrated, Benedick accuses them of having killed an innocent lady and departs. Claudio and Don Pedro decide that Benedick is in earnest and marvel at his loss of common sense.

At this moment Dogberry and Verges enter with Borachio and Conrade in custody. Having heard that Don John has fled Messina, Don Pedro expresses surprise that his two followers remain under arrest. When Don Pedro tries to ascertain from Dogberry what has taken place, Borachio suddenly breaks down and confesses the details of the plot against Hero. While Don Pedro comments on the treachery and villainy of his half brother, Claudio bemoans the death of Hero.

Leonato and Antonio appear with the Sexton, who has informed them of the exposure of the crime. Borachio assumes sole responsibility for the slander, but Leonato sarcastically identifies Don Pedro, Claudio, and Don John as accomplices. Finally accepting Don Pedro's and Claudio's protestations of innocence, Leonato commands them to declare Hero's blamelessness throughout Messina and to place an epitaph on her grave; he adds that, although he cannot restore Hero to life, Claudio may atone for his offense by marrying Antonio's daughter, who is "Almost the copy of" Hero. Claudio gladly assents, and Leonato prepares to bring Borachio face to face with Margaret, whom Borachio tries to clear of complicity. The parties go their several ways as Leonato rewards Dogberry for faithful service, and Claudio resolves to mourn one night for Hero.

V,ii. Leonato's Orchard

Finding himself unable to compose a love poem for Beatrice, Benedick dispatches Margaret to fetch her. Beatrice appears, demands to know what Benedick has done with Claudio, and quarrels with him when she learns that he has not carried out his promise to avenge Hero. After Ursula comes to tell them of the discovery of Hero's innocence, they leave to learn all the news.

V,iii. A Churchyard

Don Pedro and Claudio, with candle-bearers and musicians, hang the epitaph on Hero's supposed tomb, listen to the musicians render a song, and depart to prepare for Claudio's wedding with Leonato's fictional niece.

V,iv. Leonato's House

To Friar Francis, Antonio, and Benedick, Leonato affirms the innocence of Hero and instructs the women (Hero, Beatrice, Ursula, and Margaret) to withdraw and return masked when he sends for them. Leonato then tells Antonio to act as father of Hero and to give her as his daughter to Claudio. Benedick asks and receives permission to marry Beatrice.

Don Pedro and Claudio enter, and Antonio leaves to fetch Hero. Antonio shortly returns with the four masked ladies. Claudio accepts the hand of his new bride, but Antonio refuses to permit him to see her until he swears to wed her in front of Friar Francis. After Claudio vows to marry her, Hero unmasks and Leonato explains that Hero "died . . . but whiles her slander liv'd." When Beatrice and Benedick try to deny that love exists between them, Claudio and Hero produce handwritten notes in which each professes admiration for the other. As all prepare to celebrate the double wedding, a messenger enters with news that an armed force has captured Don John and is bringing him back to Messina.

THE MERRY WIVES OF WINDSOR
[1597–1601]¹

CHARACTERS

SIR JOHN FALSTAFF [*Mother Prat, Herne the Hunter*].

FENTON, a young gentleman.

[*Robert*] SHALLOW, a country justice.

[*Abraham*] SLENDER, cousin to *Shallow*.

[*Frank*] FORD [Brook], [*George*] PAGE, } gentlemen of Windsor.

WILLIAM PAGE, a boy, son to *Page*.

SIR HUGH EVANS, a Welsh parson.

DOCTOR CAIUS, a French physician.

HOST of the Garter Inn.

BARDOLPH, PISTOL [*Hobgoblin*], NYM, } followers of *Falstaff*.

ROBIN, page to *Falstaff*.

[*Peter*] SIMPLE, servant to *Slender*.

JOHN RUGBY, servant to *Doctor Caius*.

MISTRESS [*Alice*] FORD.

MISTRESS [*Meg*] PAGE.

ANNE PAGE, her daughter.

MISTRESS QUICKLY, servant to *Doctor Caius*.

Servants to *Page, Ford*, etc.

Scene: *Windsor, and the Neighborhood*

I,i, Windsor. In Front of Page's House

Shallow, seconded and echoed by Slender, announces to Sir Hugh Evans his intention of summoning Falstaff into court for trespassing and deer poaching. As a churchman, Sir Hugh offers to effect a compromise between Shallow and Falstaff; in an effort to divert and

---

¹ Although some editors date this comedy as early as 1597, the majority place it between *Much Ado about Nothing* and *As You Like It*.

placate Shallow, Evans suggests that they promote a marriage between Slender and Anne Page, heiress to seven hundred pounds and other resources. Unwilling to tell a lie, Evans then admits to Shallow that Falstaff is in Page's house.

In response to Sir Hugh's knocking, Page appears and thanks Shallow for his gift of venison. Acknowledging that Falstaff is within, Page tells Shallow that Falstaff has partially confessed his offense against the Justice. At this point, Falstaff approaches with Bardolph, Nym, and Pistol.

After Falstaff admits his guilt but warns Shallow that the Justice may incur public ridicule if he presses the case, Slender accuses Falstaff's cronies of making him drunk and robbing him—a charge they flatly deny. Anne Page appears with wine, Mistress Page and Mistress Ford accompanying her. Page asks his wife to invite the gentlemen to "a hot venison pasty" dinner, where he trusts they "shall drink down all unkindness." Many of the party move indoors. Shallow and Evans persuade Slender to become a suitor for the hand of Anne, who now comes to call them to dinner. Evans and Shallow leave.

Vowing that he is not hungry, Slender sends Simple (who has arrived earlier) after Shallow and then begins boasting to Anne of his wealth and experiences. When Page himself comes to take Slender to dinner, the new suitor consents to follow the others into the house.

I,ii. In Front of Page's House

Evans gives Simple a letter to convey to Mistress Quickly, the housekeeper of Doctor Caius and the confidante of Anne. In it he seeks her aid in furthering the match between Slender and Anne.

I,iii. The Garter Inn

Falstaff says that he must dismiss some of his followers in order to reduce his expenses, and the Host immediately employs Bardolph as a tapster. After the Host and Bardolph leave, Falstaff tells Pistol and Nym that he is penniless and must turn to trickery to survive. He proposes to engage Mistress Ford in a love affair because he has heard that she controls her husband's purse. Having got a similar report of Mistress Page, he has written each of the wives a letter in the expectation that they will become infatuated with him and will relieve his monetary problems. He requests Pistol to deliver the note to Mistress Page and Nym the one to Mistress Ford. Both followers refuse to become involved. In a rage, Falstaff orders his page, Robin, to convey the letters and stamps out after the boy. Annoyed by Falstaff's treatment, Pistol and Nym resolve to reveal Falstaff's scheme to Ford and Page, the two husbands.

I,iv. Doctor Caius's House

Apprehensive lest Doctor Caius return and find a stranger in his house, Mistress Quickly sends Rugby to watch for their master while she converses with Simple about the appearance and manner of Slender. Expressing the hope that heaven will "send Anne Page no worse fortune," Mistress Quickly says that she will do what she can to support Slender's suit. Rugby reports that Doctor Caius is coming, and Mistress Quickly hides Simple in the closet.

At once, Doctor Caius commands Mistress Quickly to fetch him a green box from the closet. Ordering Rugby to prepare to accompany him, Caius looks in the closet for some herbs, discovers Simple, and hauls him forth. Learning of Evans's plan to further Slender's wooing of Anne, Doctor Caius calls for paper and begins composing a letter which he describes as a challenge to Sir Hugh and which he commands Simple to transmit to the Welsh parson. After Simple has gone, Doctor Caius declares his intention of winning Anne's hand and vows to kill and mutilate Sir Hugh. Appeasing her master with a false assurance of Anne's love for him, Mistress Quickly watches the departure of Caius and Rugby and comments to herself that no woman in Windsor knows Anne's mind better than she does or "can do more than I do with her." When Fenton appears, Mistress Quickly flatters him that his wooing of Anne prospers. She accepts Fenton's gift of money and promises to help him, but when he leaves she expresses the opinion that Anne "loves him not."

II,i. In Front of Page's House

Mistress Page is reading Falstaff's letter; she expresses her distaste for the fat knight and declares that she will get revenge on him. Mistress Ford appears on her way to confer with Mistress Page, and the women speedily discover that they have received identical letters except that "the name of Page and Ford differs." Indignantly they withdraw to plot against Falstaff as Ford and Page advance, talking with Pistol and Nym.

Easily made jealous, Ford determines to investigate Pistol's allegations, whereas Page tends to discount the reports as lies. Mistress

Page and Mistress Ford join their husbands briefly, and when Mistress Quickly appears, the two wives enlist her as their emissary to Falstaff. Left to themselves, Ford and Page exchange views on the warnings they have received.

At this point the Host and Shallow appear on their way to witness the duel between Sir Hugh and Doctor Caius. Pulling the Host to one side, Ford arranges to have himself introduced to Falstaff under the name of Brook. The Host, Shallow, and Page depart for the site of the duel. Ford, voicing his opinion that Page may "be a secure fool" and trust his wife too far, resolves to probe further into the matter.

II,ii. The Garter Inn

Refusing to give Pistol one penny, Falstaff berates him until he at last relents and inquires what more Falstaff would have of him. Robin ushers in Mistress Quickly to chat with Falstaff. Stressing the unsuccessful efforts of previous seekers of Mistress Ford's favors, Mistress Quickly tells Falstaff that the suspicious and tyrannical Master Ford will be away from home between ten and eleven and that he may call on the wife then. She likewise advises that Page seldom leaves home but that Mistress Page "hopes there will come a time." Mistress Quickly assures Falstaff that neither Mistress Page nor Mistress Ford knows of the other's interest in him and adds that Mistress Page wishes Falstaff to send her Robin to serve as a go-between. Falstaff gives Mistress Quickly a reward and orders Robin to accompany her. Pistol, who has overheard the conversation and sees a chance to profit by it, leaves to intercept Mistress Quickly. While Falstaff rejoices over his good prospects, Bardolph brings him a cup of sack as an introduction from Brook (Ford in disguise), who follows on Bardolph's heels.

In confidence, Brook tells Falstaff that he has invested a large amount of money in an unsuccessful attempt to promote a love affair with Mistress Ford. Having heard that she has received the attentions of other men while spurning him, Brook enlists Falstaff's assistance in testing Mistress Ford's honor. To this end he offers Falstaff an open expense account. Falstaff says that he has an appointment with Mistress Ford, guarantees to deliver her into Brook's power, professes that his primary interest in the good wife is her husband's money, and promises Brook that he will gain the favors of his ladylove. When Brook suggests that Falstaff might wish to avoid Ford, Falstaff boastfully states that he will "stare him out of his wits" and "awe him" with his cudgel. Now certain of his wife's double-dealing, "Brook" starts planning to expose the plot.

II,iii. A Field near Windsor

Caius, accompanied by Rugby, believes that Evans has failed to meet him for the duel. Eager to demonstrate his prowess with a rapier, Doctor Caius orders Rugby to defend himself. As Rugby protests, the Host, Shallow, Slender, and Page come on the scene. While the Host humorously praises Doctor Caius, Shallow reminds the doctor that Parson Evans has proved himself the wiser man by declining the fight. Getting rid of the other witnesses, the Host suggests to Caius that he go directly to Frogmore where, with the Host's assistance, he can woo Mistress Anne for himself.

III,i. A Field near Frogmore

Although he asks Simple to search for Doctor Caius, Evans admits to himself that he is nervous and would be glad if Caius did not appear. Simple returns with news that Caius is approaching, and Evans starts reading a book. In the meantime, Page, Shallow, and Slender enter. Professing readiness to discard his book for the sword, Evans denounces Caius as an impostor and quack. Upon the arrival of the Host, Caius, and Rugby, Page and Shallow manage to keep the rivals apart. In midst of the angry confusion, the Host confesses that he directed the duelists "to wrong places," and so neither can blame the other for failing the appointment. Left to themselves, Caius and Evans drop their quarrel and join forces to contrive revenge on the Host, who has made them laughingstocks.

III,ii. A Street in Windsor

On her way with Robin to see Mistress Ford, Mistress Page meets Ford. Learning that Robin is in the service of Falstaff, Ford grows surer of uncovering proof of Falstaff's philandering with his own wife and Mistress Page. Certain that he will find Falstaff at his house, Ford starts to follow Mistress Page and Robin but meets Page, Shallow, and the others on their way to dine with Mistress Anne. Page indicates that Slender has his approval as a suitor for his daughter but says that his wife prefers Doctor Caius. In reply to the Host's specific question, Page says that he does not approve of Fenton because the young man has no estate and has been a companion of Prince Hal and Poins. If Anne chooses Fenton, she will have to marry him without a dowry.

Promising to show his guests a monster, Ford persuades some of them to accompany him to dinner. Shallow and Slender continue to Master Page's, where they will "have the freer wooing."

III,iii. Ford's House

Mistress Ford and Mistress Page instruct John and Robert, the two servants, on how, upon call, they are to remove the large basket soiled with the lye and suds from dirty linen and empty it in the muddy ditch near the Thames. As the servants depart, Robin informs the two wives that Falstaff has arrived through the back door. Robin vows that he has kept faith with the women and leaves; Mistress Page hides herself. Coming in and believing himself alone with Mistress Ford, Falstaff says that he wishes Ford were dead so that he could marry her. He protests his love for her, and she insists that she is unworthy to be his lady. When she inquires if he loves Mistress Page, Falstaff indignantly denies such perfidy.

Robin enters to announce the sudden arrival of Mistress Page, whereupon Falstaff hides himself behind the arras. Loudly Mistress Page tells her friend that Ford is approaching "with all the officers in Windsor" to look for the gentleman he suspects of trifling with his wife. Mistress Ford admits that she has such a visitor and says that she is more concerned about his safety than about her own reputation. Mistress Page suggests that Mistress Ford conceal him in the basket and thus convey him outside the house, but Mistress Ford says that he is too large to get into it. Stepping forth, Falstaff squeezes himself into the basket while the women cover him with foul linen. Picking up the "buck-basket" with Falstaff in it, the servants leave as Ford, Page, Caius, and Evans enter.

Locking the door, Ford invites his friends to help him search the house. While the men are out of the room, Mistress Ford and Mistress Page gloat over the trick they have played on Falstaff and congratulate themselves that Ford will find nothing to confirm his jealousy. They decide to apologize to Falstaff in order that they may "betray him to another punishment." Returning from their fruitless search of the house, Ford's friends chide him for his baseless mistrust of his wife. Page invites his friends to breakfast and hawking on the following morning.

III,iv. In Front of Page's House

Fenton admits to Anne that her father's wealth induced him to court her, but he vehemently insists that he now woos her for her true virtues. Anne urges him to persevere in his efforts to win her father's approval. They step aside to continue their conversation as Shallow, Slender, and Mistress Quickly enter.

Shallow and Mistress Quickly are trying to overcome Slender's timidity as a suitor, and Mistress Quickly asks Anne to listen to him. Commenting,

> This is my father's choice.
> O, what a world of vile ill-favour'd faults
> Looks handsome in three hundred pounds a year!

Anne reluctantly joins them. After Slender paraphrases Shallow's speeches to Anne, she says,

> Good Master Shallow, let him woo for himself.

This task proves too much for Slender, who tells her that the match is Shallow's and Page's scheme rather than his own. Page enters with his wife, instructs Anne to accept Slender, and rebukes Fenton. Mistress Page also tells Fenton that he is unwelcome.

When Page, Shallow, and Slender depart, Mistress Quickly advises Fenton to plead his case with Mistress Page. After Anne implores her mother not to marry her to Slender, Mistress Page declares that she seeks a better husband for her daughter, and Mistress Quickly identifies this man as Doctor Caius. When Anne says that she would prefer being implanted in the earth and pelted to death with turnips, her mother reassures her and tells Fenton that she will determine Anne's own wishes and consent to them. Talking privately with Fenton, Mistress Quickly claims credit for furthering his cause. He thanks her, commissions her to deliver a ring to Anne, and rewards her. Left to herself, Mistress Quickly expresses the wish that every one of Anne's three suitors may prove successful; she has promised to do what she can for all three, and she will be as good as her word, "but speciously for Master Fenton."

III,v. The Garter Inn

While Bardolph fetches sack, Falstaff laments the indignity of the buck-basket episode and resolves that he will not be the victim of another such trick. Bardolph ushers in Mistress Quickly and leaves to prepare more sack for the thirsty knight.

In face of protests from Falstaff that he has seen enough of Mistress Ford, Mistress Quickly informs him that Master Ford has gone bird-hunting and that the good wife wishes Falstaff to visit her.

Falstaff agrees; Mistress Quickly scurries out; and Ford enters, disguised as Brook.

With mounting indignation, Falstaff relates how Mistress Ford and Mistress Page arranged for his escape from Ford's house in the buck-basket. Brook asks Falstaff if he will now abandon his pursuit of Mistress Ford, but Falstaff tells him of his new rendezvous, promises Brook that he will make a cuckold of Ford, and hastens toward Ford's house. All of his suspicions and jealousy again aroused, Ford determines to catch Falstaff red-handed.

IV,i. A Street in Windsor

Mistress Page, conducting her son William to school, meets Mistress Quickly and Evans, and the parson says that Slender has dismissed school. At Mistress Page's request, Evans drills William in his Latin. Finally the lesson ends, Evans and William leave, and Mistress Page goes off with Mistress Quickly, who has told her that Mistress Ford is awaiting Falstaff.

IV,ii. Ford's House

Falstaff resumes his courting of Mistress Ford, but Mistress Page arrives, and Falstaff must hide in an adjoining room. Speaking loudly for Falstaff's benefit, Mistress Page tells her friend that Ford has learned of the recent visit of her lover and of his escape, that he suspects Falstaff has returned, and that he is coming with his companions to apprehend the knight in the act. Confessing that Falstaff is present, Mistress Ford asks what she can do to save their lives.

Emerging from his concealment, Falstaff says that he will not go near the basket again and suggests a variety of hiding places, all of which Mistress Ford vetoes as futile. The two wives finally decide to disguise Falstaff as the fat old witch of Brainford. To confuse her husband further, Mistress Ford orders the two servants to carry out the buck-basket as they had done before.

Ford, tramping in with Page, Shallow, Caius, and Evans, stops the servants and pulls all the linen from the basket. In spite of remonstrances from his wife and friends, Ford institutes another search of the house. Outraged when Mistress Page brings down Mother Prat, the witch of Brainford (Falstaff in woman's clothes), Ford beats the fat creature out of the house. Still suspicious, Ford persuades his companions to continue their investigation. Exulting in the drubbing Falstaff has received, the two wives decide to tell their husbands all that has happened and to encourage them to arrange for a public shaming of Falstaff.

IV,iii. The Garter Inn

Bardolph tells the Host that certain Germans wish to rent three horses in order to meet a Duke from their country. The Host agrees but indicates that he will overcharge them.[1]

IV,iv. Ford's House

Page, Ford, their wives, and Evans plot public sport at Falstaff's expense. Mistress Page recalls the tale of Herne the Hunter, who, with "great ragg'd horns" on his head, haunts Windsor Forest. The pranksters thereupon decide to lure Falstaff, disguised like Herne and with "huge horns on his head," to meet the wives at Herne's Oak. When the fat knight appears, the wives will flee, and children will, in the manner of fairies, surround Falstaff, pinch him, and burn him with their tapers until he tells the truth about his escapades. Then the adults will mock him home to Windsor. Mistress Page plans to dress Anne in white as Queen of the Fairies and resolves that Doctor Caius will marry her daughter. Master Page, thinking that Slender may steal Anne away and marry her at Eton, agrees to furnish the cloth. Evans volunteers to instruct the children in their roles.

IV,v. The Garter Inn

Slender has sent Simple to inquire of the witch of Brainford whether Nym has his chain and whether he will prosper in his wooing of Anne. Falstaff pretends to relay noncommittal answers to Simple, who departs satisfied.

Bardolph enters and informs the Host that the three Germans have stolen his horses, just as Evans comes to warn the Host to beware of the same rogues. Caius follows immediately to tell the Host that no one at court knows of any German Duke. Crying that he has been undone, the Host beseeches Falstaff to help him and rushes out with Bardolph. In a short solilioquy, Falstaff wishes that all the world might be deceived as he has been and says that if he had enough breath to say his prayers he would repent. Mistress

---

[1] Most editors agree that this brief scene is all that remains of a more elaborate one in which Caius and Evans punish the Host by having Pistol, Nym, and Rugby impersonate Germans and run off with the Host's horses. Possibly Ford and Shallow later contrive to attach the blame to Falstaff.

Quickly appears and persuades him, in spite of his resolutions, to receive another message from the two wives.

IV,vi. The Garter Inn

Fenton has received a letter from Anne in which she tells of the plans to shame Falstaff at Herne's Oak at midnight; she also reveals that she has agreed with her father to elope with Slender and with her mother to go with Doctor Caius; but she says that her true wish is to marry Fenton. The young man promises the Host a hundred pounds in gold if he will have a priest ready at the church to marry them between twelve and one. The Host agrees to arrange for the priest.

V,i. The Garter Inn

Placing his faith in the good omen of the number three, Falstaff consents to wear the horns and chain that Mistress Quickly will supply. She leaves, and Ford appears in his disguise as Brook. For the third time promising Brook to promote his affair with Mistress Ford, Falstaff describes the beating he received from Master Ford, who "hath the finest mad devil of jealousy in him."

V,ii. Windsor Park

Page, Shallow, and Slender conceal themselves to await the tormenting of Falstaff, and Page counsels Slender to remember his forthcoming elopement with Anne. Shallow reminds his cousin that Anne will wear white apparel.

V,iii. In the Vicinity of Windsor Park

Mistress Page tells Mistress Ford and Doctor Caius that Anne will be in a green habit instead of the white one that her father and Slender expect her to wear. Caius leaves, and the two wives hurry to observe the shaming of Falstaff.

V,iv. Windsor Park

Evans, dressed like a satyr, leads his group of "fairies" to their appointed place.

V,v. Windsor Park

Disguised like Herne and wearing a buck's head, Falstaff invokes Jove's aid in his lecherous designs. The two wives meet him, and Falstaff says that they may divide him and he will bequeath his horns to their husbands. At the sound of horns blowing, Mistress Ford and Mistress Page run off.

With Evans in the guise of a satyr, the fairies, including Pistol as Hobgoblin and Anne as the Fairy Queen, gather round Falstaff, who lies down on his face. Joining hands, the fairies circle the tree and singe Falstaff's fingers with their tapers. They then pinch him while they dance and sing.

During the song, Doctor Caius leads away a fairy in green, Slender takes off one in white, and Fenton leaves with Anne. At the sound of hunters, the fairies disappear, and Falstaff removes his buck's head and rises. The Pages and the Fords now confront Falstaff and taunt him. Falstaff begins to perceive that he is "made an ass," and Evans reminds him that if he served God and abandoned his fleshly desires, fairies would not pinch him. Dejected and crestfallen, Falstaff says that they may use him as they wish.

While the conversation continues, Slender returns to report that when he unmasked his white fairy in the Eton church he discovered that he had eloped with a great lubberly boy. Mistress Page explains to her bewildered husband that she changed the color of Anne's garments so that Doctor Caius could identify her and wed her at the deanery. At this instant Doctor Cauis storms up with the news that he has married a peasant boy in green.

Fenton and Anne appear to satisfy Ford's curiosity and answer Page's misgivings. Fenton announces that he and Anne are lawfully married and that their deception has enabled Anne to avoid "A thousand irreligious cursed hours/Which forced marriage would have brought upon her." Ford cynically comments that this is no remedy, but Page wishes Fenton joy and says that "What cannot be eschew'd must be embrac'd." Mistress Page adds her blessing on the couple, and Ford tells Falstaff that his promise to Master Brook will come true because that night Master Brook will "lie with Mistress Ford."

AS YOU LIKE IT [1599–1600]

CHARACTERS

DUKE SENIOR, living in banishment.

DUKE FREDERICK, his brother, and usurper of his dominions.

AMIENS,
JAQUES, } lords attending on the banished *Duke*.

LE BEAU, a courtier attending on *Duke Frederick*.

CHARLES, wrestler to *Duke Frederick*.

OLIVER,
JAQUES, } sons of Sir Rowland
ORLANDO, } de Boys.

ADAM,
DENNIS, } servants to *Oliver*.

TOUCHSTONE, a clown.

SIR OLIVER MARTEXT, a vicar.

CORIN,
SILVIUS, } shepherds.

WILLIAM, a country fellow, in love with *Audrey*.

A Person representing *Hymen*.

ROSALIND [GANYMEDE], daughter to the banished *Duke*.

CELIA [ALIENA], daughter to *Duke Frederick*.

PHEBE, a shepherdess.

AUDREY, a country wench.

Lords, Pages, Foresters, and Attendants.

Scene: *Oliver's House; Duke Frederick's Court; the Forest of Arden*

I,i. Orchard of Oliver's House

Orlando is complaining to Adam of the shabby treatment he receives from his oldest brother, Oliver. Oliver has sent his other brother, Jaques, to school, but he has insisted on Orlando's remaining at home without proper education and without suitable support. Oliver comes up, and the two brothers quarrel to the point of exchanging blows. Orlando asks Oliver to give him his meager inheritance and let him depart. Grudgingly Oliver agrees to let Orlando have a part of his request and dismisses him along with Adam, who has tried to mediate the brothers' disagreement.

Resolved to rid himself of his brother, Oliver orders Dennis to call in Charles, Duke Frederick's professional wrestler, who has come on urgent business. At Oliver's request, Charles gives a brief recital of court news. Banished by his brother, Duke Senior with three or four loyal courtiers has taken voluntary exile in the Forest of Arden, where he and his companions are attracting additional followers and are leading an idyllic existence. Duke Senior's daughter Rosalind, on the insistence of her devoted cousin Celia, remains at the court of the usurper, who is exploiting the estate of his older brother.

Charles then comes to the purpose of his visit. He has heard that Orlando plans to disguise himself and challenge Charles in a wrestling match. Because Charles will be defending his title, he fears that he may injure the inexperienced youth, and he implores Oliver to dissuade Orlando from his rash intention. Seeing an opportunity to destroy Orlando, Oliver thanks Charles for this show of friendship but proceeds to describe Orlando as a treacherous villain and says, "I had as lief thou didst break his neck as his finger." With a clear conscience, Charles declares that he will handle Orlando brutally if the young man appears on the morrow. After Charles leaves, Oliver admits that he is jealous of Orlando's virtues and popularity. In expectation of Charles's inflicting permanent injury on the challenger, Oliver will encourage Orlando to go ahead with the match.

I,ii. A Lawn in Front of Duke Frederick's Palace

Celia chides Rosalind for being in low spirits over her father's banishment. In an effort to throw off her sadness, Rosalind responds to Celia's plea that she "be merry" by suggesting that they amuse themselves by talking about love. While they are chatting, Touchstone comes to summon Celia to her father. The two girls exchange jests with the Clown, and Le Beau approaches with the news that they "have lost much good sport" by not seeing the wrestling. He describes how Charles has defeated three brothers in succession and inflicted mortal injury on all of them. Touchstone questions that such violence is proper sport for ladies to witness. The arrival of Duke Frederick, Orlando, Charles, and the court for the next match interrupts their discussion. On learning that Rosalind and Celia wish to watch the bout, Duke Frederick tells them that he has tried to discourage Orlando from risking certain defeat and asks the girls to add their pleas to his. Orlando listens courteously but persists in undertaking his trial of strength. The cousins give Orlando their best wishes, and Duke Frederick limits the match to one fall. After a brief tussle Orlando throws Charles. Protesting that he is "not yet well breath'd," Orlando is eager to continue, but Charles is carried out unable to speak.

Learning that Orlando is the son of Sir Rowland de Boys, his former enemy, Duke Frederick commends the youth for his gallantry but wishes that he could claim another father and petulantly departs. Celia is embarrassed by her father's surliness, and Rosalind, who identifies Sir Rowland as a onetime friend of Duke Senior, praises Orlando and gives him a chain from her neck. Implying that Orlando has won her heart as well as his match with Charles, Rosalind goes out with Celia. Orlando also is aware of an unusual emotion; but as he ponders, Le Beau comes to advise him to leave immediately because Duke Frederick "is humorous" and has conceived an intense mistrust of and dislike for the young victor. Orlando thanks Le Beau and prepares to follow his counsel but not before he learns several details about the two girls and reveals that he has fallen in love with Rosalind.

I,iii. A Room in Duke Frederick's Palace

Celia, somewhat astonished at Rosalind's sudden infatuation for Orlando, is teasing her cousin and asks if she can seriously love Sir Rowland's youngest son. While they are talking, Duke Frederick enters with his attending lords and tells Rosalind that within the next ten days she must, on pain of death, remove herself farther than twenty miles from his court. Ignoring Rosalind's appeal for an explanation, the Duke says that he does not trust her and that he would have banished her sooner had it not been for Celia. He is equally deaf to Celia's intervention on Rosalind's behalf. He calls his daughter a fool, repeats his warning to Rosalind, and leaves.

Immediately Celia assures Rosalind that she will disown her father and that they will leave court together to seek Duke Senior in the Forest of Arden. They decide that Rosalind will disguise herself as the youth Ganymede and that Celia will pose as his sister Aliena. As a companion they select Touchstone, who has been loyal to Celia.

II,i. The Forest of Arden

Philosophizing with his followers, Duke Senior emphasizes the advantages that their rigorous life in the forest provides in contrast with court life. The Duke suggests that they go on a deer hunt, and this reminds a lord of Jaques's moralizing over a wounded stag. Fond of hearing Jaques in such moods, Duke Senior asks his attendants to direct him to the melancholy lord.

II,ii. A Room in Duke Frederick's Palace

Concerned about the absence of Celia and Touchstone and informed of the two cousins' interest in Orlando, Duke Frederick sends for Oliver in the hope of recovering "these foolish runaways."

II,iii. In Front of Oliver's House

Adam warns Orlando that Oliver, jealously enraged by his younger brother's success and acclaim, plans to kill him that very night. Without means of financing his flight, Orlando replies that he has no place to go and would do better to stay and risk the hatred of his brother. Generously, Adam gives Orlando the five hundred crowns he has saved during more than sixty years of domestic service and offers to accompany him.

II,iv. The Forest of Arden

Tired from their journey, Ganymede (Rosalind), Aliena (Celia), and Touchstone arrive in the forest. While they discuss their situation, Silvius and Corin approach. Silvius, the younger of the two shepherds, is telling his older companion of his hopeless love for the disdainful Phebe and leaves to find her. Ganymede and Touchstone, moved by Silvius's lament, begin a conversation on their own difficulties in love, but Aliena interrupts with the suggestion that they seek food from Corin. To Ganymede's inquiry, Corin answers that he is shepherd to another man who wishes to sell his cottage, sheep, and pasturage. Silvius has been planning to purchase the property and its assets but has neglected the matter to pursue his love affair with Phebe. Happy at their promise to retain him at better wages, Corin agrees to make the purchase for Ganymede and Aliena.

II,v. Another Part of the Forest of Arden

Amiens sings "Under the greenwood tree," and Jaques demands that he continue. While they prepare the dinner table for the Duke, they join in another lyric. Then Jaques, who "can suck melancholy out of a song, as a weasel sucks eggs," renders an air of his own.

II,vi. The Forest

Adam and Orlando have also gained the cover of the forest. The
old man is faint, fatigued, and resigned to death. Orlando attempts
to rally his companion and promises to find him shelter and food.

II,vii. The Forest

Hearing that the usually melancholy Jaques has been singing,
Duke Senior wishes to talk with him, and he appears before the
messenger leaves. Jaques has met Touchstone in the forest and has
been so greatly impressed with the Clown's mixture of humor and
wisdom that he asks Duke Senior for "a motley coat." While Duke
Senior and Jaques moralize, Orlando dashes up with his sword drawn.
Declaring himself famished, Orlando demands that the group supply
his needs before proceeding with their own meal. Shamed by Duke
Senior's courteous welcome, Orlando sheathes his sword, apologizes
for his gruffness, and leaves to fetch Adam to the feast. The incident
prompts Jaques to deliver his famous speech, "All the world's a
stage,/And all the men and women merely players." Orlando returns
with Adam in his arms; Amiens entertains the diners with a song;
and Duke Senior welcomes Orlando and Adam as members of the
household of his former friend, "good Sir Rowland."

III,i. Duke Frederick's Palace

Duke Frederick commands Oliver to produce Orlando dead or
alive within twelve months or face banishment and loss of all his
property. Oliver protests that he has never loved his brother, but
the Duke calls him a villain and orders his officers to prepare to
appropriate Oliver's "house and lands."

III,ii. The Forest

Orlando is wandering through the forest hanging poems to Rosalind on the trees. He departs, and Touchstone enters with Corin. The
Clown bewilders the old shepherd with his humorously philosophical
comparison of pastoral life with court life. While they are talking,
Ganymede appears reading one of Orlando's poems. Touchstone
teases Rosalind by extemporaneously composing a parody of the
verse. As the Clown and Rosalind banter over the rhymes, Aliena
(Celia) comes in reading another lyric. Sending Touchstone and
Corin away, the two girls discuss the poetry they have found. Aliena
has seen Orlando with Rosalind's chain about his neck, and when

she identifies the young wrestler as the author of the poetry, Ganymede's spontaneous wish is to discard her male disguise and return to proper feminine attire and character. Before they can settle on a course of action, Orlando and Jaques walk up, and the two girls step aside.

In his blunt, dour manner, Jaques requests Orlando to "mar no more trees with writing love songs in their barks." After an exchange of raillery, Jaques tells Orlando that his worst fault is to be in love and leaves him. Ganymede and Aliena step forward, and Ganymede engages Orlando in a "catechism" on Time. Orlando finds Ganymede's speech surprisingly refined for the rural setting of which he claims to be a native. Ganymede explains this quality by saying he received early instruction from "an old religious uncle." Then Ganymede speaks contemptuously of love and especially of some man who has been carving "Rosalind" in the bark of trees and scattering poems addressed to her. When Orlando confesses that he is the man, Ganymede insists that Orlando exhibits none of the symptoms of "a man in love." Ganymede goes on to assert that "Love is merely madness" and that he can cure Orlando by assuming the role of Rosalind in a series of daily meetings. At first Orlando does not wish to be cured, but when Ganymede suggests that Orlando address him as Rosalind and woo him daily, he agrees. From now on, Ganymede says, "you must call me Rosalind."

III,iii. The Forest

Jaques overhears Touchstone's whimsical proposal of wedlock to Audrey, with whom the Clown is waiting for Sir Oliver Martext, the "hedge-priest" who has promised to marry them. Sir Oliver appears and insists that some man give Audrey in marriage. Jaques at first offers to "give her" but quickly advises the couple to find a reputable priest who can officiate properly. In an aside, Touchstone admits that he would prefer a questionable ceremony so that he might have a possible excuse to leave his wife, but he thinks better of the scheme and with Audrey accompanies Jaques to find a qualified clergyman.

III,iv. The Forest

Rosalind and Celia, still impersonating Ganymede and Aliena, are discussing Orlando's tardiness in keeping his appointment. While they wait, Rosalind tells of an encounter with Duke Senior, who failed to recognize Ganymede as his daughter. Corin calls them to watch the disdainful Phebe spurn the suit of Silvius.

III,v. Another Part of the Forest

Ganymede, Aliena, and Corin eavesdrop while Silvius vainly implores Phebe to show him a small amount of pity and love. Ganymede intervenes and roundly berates Phebe for her unwarranted pride and contempt, but Phebe promptly falls in love with Ganymede. Warning Phebe against this and advising her to show more favor to Silvius, Ganymede retires with Aliena and Corin. Quoting a line from Marlowe's *Hero and Leander*, Phebe declares that she cannot love Silvius but will accept his company and friendship. After describing Ganymede, Phebe says that she has more cause to hate the youth than to love him and persuades Silvius to bear him a letter.

IV,i. The Forest

While Ganymede and Jaques are analyzing the latter's particular brand of melancholy, Orlando joins them, and Ganymede quickly gets rid of Jaques. Turning to Orlando, Ganymede chides him for being late and accuses him of being insincere in his professed love of Rosalind. After prompting Orlando to propose marriage and then rejecting him, Ganymede says that he will play Rosalind in "a more coming-on disposition" and directs Aliena to marry them in a mock ceremony. They then chat about the future of their married lives until Orlando excuses himself for two hours to "attend the Duke at dinner." Pretending to be vexed with Orlando, Ganymede goads him into vowing to return by two o'clock. Orlando leaves, and Ganymede confesses to Aliena that "she" is "many fathom deep" in love.

IV,ii. The Forest

Jaques and other lords are bearing a slain deer to the Duke and sing to celebrate their success.

IV,iii. The Forest

Ganymede and Aliena are talking about Orlando's failure to return at two o'clock. Silvius delivers Phebe's letter to Ganymede. Ganymede tells Silvius that it consists of a masculine diatribe against a rival suitor, but the shepherd denies that he invented the letter or wrote it. Ganymede then reads Phebe's shameless declaration of love for him and reveals her exploitation of Silvius. Ganymede sends the jilted lover back to Phebe with instructions that if she loves Ganymede she is to love Silvius also.

At this moment, Oliver appears looking for Ganymede's cottage. Assured that he is talking to Ganymede, Oliver relates how Orlando, in rescuing him from a "suck'd and hungry lioness," incurred a severe wound on the arm. After commiting Oliver to Duke Senior's care, Orlando fainted but recovered and dispatched Oliver with the bloody bandage to make his excuses to Ganymede. Ganymede swoons but quickly rallies to the anxious questioning of Oliver and Aliena. When Oliver teases Ganymede for fainting at the sight of blood, the youth boasts that this is merely part of his pretending to be Orlando's Rosalind but admits, "I should have been a woman by right."

V,i. The Forest

Audrey is insisting to Touchstone that Sir Oliver was competent to marry them, but the Clown assures her that they will find a time and urges her to be patient. They meet William, a bumpkin in love with Audrey. Touchstone befuddles William with his wit and convinces him that he should abandon his courtship of the wench. Corin summons Touchstone to Ganymede and Aliena.

V,ii. The Forest

Oliver, madly in love with Aliena, implores Orlando to help him in his suit and promises to make Orlando heir to their father's estate. If he can win Aliena, Oliver will "here live and die a shepherd." Orlando agrees and says that he will invite the Duke to the wedding on the morrow. Oliver departs as Ganymede approaches. Orlando confesses to Ganymede that the new-found happiness of Oliver and Aliena makes him sad to think of his own frustrated love of Rosalind. Ganymede asks if he cannot continue to play the role of Rosalind, but Orlando says that he "can no longer live by thinking." Ganymede declares that he is skilled in benevolent magic and promises that Orlando will marry Rosalind when Oliver weds Aliena.

At this instant, Phebe and Silvius confront Ganymede. Phebe is indignant over Ganymede's showing of her letter to Silvius. After a series of avowals of love by each person present, Ganymede finally guarantees that each of the others will have his heart's desire on the following day, although fulfillment seems to them patently impossible.

V,iii. The Forest

Touchstone promises Audrey that they will be married the next day, and they listen while two of Duke Senior's pages sing an "untuneable" ditty.

V,iv. The Forest

In the presence of his court, Duke Senior asks Orlando if he believes that Ganymede can do all that he has promised. Orlando, somewhat dubiously, professes hope. Ganymede, Silvius, and Phebe appear. Duke Senior assures Ganymede that he is willing to bestow Rosalind on Orlando, and Orlando reaffirms his wish to marry her. Phebe also vows to marry Silvius if she refuses to wed Ganymede, and Silvius states that he will still have Phebe. Adjuring all to keep their words, Ganymede and Aliena withdraw to implement the solution. Duke Senior sees in Ganymede "Some lively touches of [his] daughter's favour," and Orlando confesses that he thought Ganymede might be Rosalind's brother before he told his history. Touchstone and Audrey arrive, and the Clown requests permission to marry Audrey. His droll and "sententious" speech stimulates Jaques to interrogate him on the "seventh cause" of a quarrel, and Touchstone delivers a declamation on the seven "degrees of the lie," a satirical attack on the code of duelling.

As Touchstone completes his analysis of "the lie," Rosalind, Celia, and Hymen appear to the accompaniment of soft music. After Hymen in a song presents Rosalind in her true character to her father, Duke Senior and Orlando gladly welcome her. Phebe realizes that she has lost Ganymede. In a second song Hymen honors the approaching nuptials of Orlando and Rosalind, Oliver and Celia, Silvius and Phebe, and Touchstone and Audrey.

Jaques de Boys, the second of Sir Rowland's sons, interrupts with the news that Duke Frederick, after heading a force to capture Duke Senior in the forest, has met "an old religious man," repented of his violent purposes, and has restored the crown to Duke Senior and all estates to his faithful attendants. Indicating that he will confer "a potent dukedom" on Orlando, Duke Senior welcomes Jaques de Boys and calls on all the court to celebrate "the good of our returned fortune."

After confirming the report that Duke Frederick has forsaken the pomp of court and entered a religious order, Jaques the Melancholy announces that he will join the former usurper and become a "convertite." To the Duke, Jaques "bequeaths" a propitious return to his previous "honour"; to Orlando, Oliver, and Silvius he wills happy and successful marriages; to Touchstone he grants two months of wrangling. Finding "dancing measures" distasteful, Jaques retires to Duke Senior's "abandon'd cave" to await the ruler's final instructions.

Epilogue

Rosalind artfully reminds the audience of her masculine disguise [1] and requests their applause and approval.

[1] The Epilogue possibly also reminds the audience that a boy actor has played the role of the heroine.

TWELFTH NIGHT [1] [1599–1602]

CHARACTERS

ORSINO, Duke of Illyria.

SEBASTIAN, a young gentleman, brother to *Viola*.

ANTONIO, a sea captain, friend to *Sebastian*.

A SEA CAPTAIN, friend to *Viola*.

VALENTINE, CURIO, } gentlemen attending on *Orsino*.

SIR TOBY BELCH, uncle to *Olivia*.

SIR ANDREW AGUECHEEK.

MALVOLIO, steward to *Olivia*.

FABIAN, FESTE [*Sir Topas*], a clown, } servants to *Olivia*.

OLIVIA, a rich countess.

VIOLA [CESARIO], sister of *Sebastian*.

MARIA, *Olivia's* waiting woman.

Lords, a Priest, Sailors, Musicians, and Attendants.

Scene: *A City in Illyria; and the Nearby Seacoast*

I,i. The Duke's Palace

Orsino is consoling himself with music. When Curio inquires if he would like to hunt, Orsino replies that he would more gladly pursue Olivia, to whom he has sent Valentine as an emissary. Valentine returns with word that Olivia is determined to mourn her brother's death and to lead a life of seclusion for seven years. Orsino rhapsodizes on how a girl of such sensitivity would express her emotions toward a sweetheart.

I,ii. The Seacoast

Congratulating Viola on her escape from drowning after the loss of their ship in a violent storm, the Sea Captain tells her that he saw her brother, Sebastian, tie himself to a mast and float away. From

---

[1] The play's full title is *Twelfth Night; or What You Will.*

the Captain, Viola also learns that she has landed in Illyria and that the country's ruler, Orsino, is a bachelor in love with the grief-stricken Olivia. Viola asks the Captain to introduce her, disguised as a eunuch, to Orsino.

I,iii. Olivia's House

Maria is attempting to warn Sir Toby of Olivia's displeasure at his heavy drinking and boisterous behavior and of her exception to Sir Andrew Aguecheek, "a very fool and a prodigal," whom Sir Toby is sponsoring as a suitor for her hand. Sir Toby describes Sir Andrew as wealthy, musical, and fluent in three or four languages. Maria insists that Sir Toby's crony is a fool, coward, and habitual drunkard.

When Sir Andrew joins them, there follows a brief exchange of jests, most of them at Sir Andrew's expense. Maria leaves, and the two men discuss Sir Andrew's prospects as a wooer of Olivia. Sir Andrew has become discouraged and has resolved to leave, but Sir Toby persuades him to prolong his visit for another month. Their conversation reveals Sir Toby's mischievous purpose to exploit the gullible, stupid, and unprepossessing knight.

I,iv. The Duke's Palace

Valentine tells Cesario (actually Viola disguised as a young man) that he has succeeded in winning Orsino's confidence and favor. Entering with Curio and other attendants, Orsino instructs Cesario to intercede with Olivia on his behalf. Although Cesario doubts that he will prove effective as an intermediary, Orsino packs him off with three or four attendants. As she departs, Viola comments to herself that she would gladly become Orsino's wife.

I,v. Olivia's House

In an exchange of quips, Maria tells Feste that Olivia is provoked with his absence. He retorts that Maria would be a good match for Sir Toby if he stopped drinking, and she flounces out. As Olivia and Malvolio walk in, Feste launches into a series of jokes that amuse Olivia in spite of herself. Olivia asks Malvolio if he agrees that Feste is improving as a clown, but the pompous and humorless steward labels Feste "a barren rascal" and marvels that anyone can find him amusing. Olivia rebukes Malvolio for taking Feste's railing seriously and tells her steward that he is "sick of self-love" and tastes "with a distemper'd appetite." Maria enters with the news that a young gentleman from Count Orsino seeks an interview with Olivia but is being detained by Sir Toby. Olivia orders Maria to send the "fair young man" away. While Maria is out on her errand, Sir Toby appears, half drunk and uncertain in speech. He departs; Feste gives a humorous description of a drunken man; and Olivia sends the Clown to arrange a legal inquiry into Sir Toby's drunkenness.

Malvolio reports the persistence, handsomeness, and youthfulness of the caller. Relenting, Olivia says that she will "once more hear Orsino's embassy" and orders Malvolio to send the visitor and Maria to her. Having assured herself that Olivia is indeed the mistress of the house, Cesario pays her a number of compliments, all the while parrying her inquiries about his own status and background. After persuading her to dismiss Maria, he forcefully presents Orsino's suit. Olivia admits Orsino's many good qualities but says that she does not and can never love the Duke. Cesario's enthusiasm and eloquence so impress her, however, that she strongly intimates that she would welcome another visit from the young messenger. Cesario declines to accept Olivia's proffered reward and departs. Intrigued with the emissary, Olivia summons Malvolio and directs him to overtake Cesario and give the youth a ring he has left behind.

II,i. The Seacoast

Sebastian, saddened by the drowning of his twin sister after the sinking of their ship, is taking his leave of Antonio, the sea captain who rescued him. Antonio desires to accompany Sebastian as his servant, but Sebastian proposes to go to Orsino's court, where Antonio has many enemies. Antonio reluctantly agrees to leave Sebastian but intimates that he will rejoin him.

II,ii. A Street

Malvolio has overtaken Cesario, who declines to receive the ring. Petulantly Malvolio tosses the ring at the page's feet and leaves. Viola now perceives that Olivia has fallen in love with an imaginary man, Cesario. Orsino loves Olivia; Viola loves Orsino; and Olivia loves Cesario. Furthermore, as long as Viola poses as Cesario she has little hope of attracting Orsino's romantic interest. Viola concludes that the knot is too hard for her to untie and that Time alone can untangle matters.

II,iii. Olivia's House

Sir Toby and Sir Andrew have continued their drunken revelry until after midnight. Feste comes in and encourages them to still more rollicking behavior. When their noise and singing increase, Maria appears to warn them that Olivia has sent Malvolio to turn them out. Haughtily, Malvolio enters and conveys Olivia's demand that they quiet down or leave the house. Offended by Sir Toby's and Feste's mockery, Malvolio reprimands Maria for bringing more wine and goes to report her insubordination to Olivia.

Resentful of Malvolio's officiousness, the roisterers applaud Maria's plot to gain revenge on the steward by forging a letter in Olivia's handwriting and thus to persuade him that his mistress is in love with him. The pranksters will then hide themselves and eavesdrop on Malvolio when he finds the note. Maria leaves, and Sir Toby persuades Sir Andrew to send for more money to finance their revels.

II,iv. The Duke's Palace

Desiring to hear a ditty that Feste sings especially well, Orsino sends Curio to fetch him. Orsino questions Cesario about his sweetheart, and Cesario describes her as being of the same age and complexion as Orsino. Orsino comments that a man should choose a wife younger than he. Curio now returns with Feste, who sings a melancholy love lyric.

Excusing everyone except Cesario, Orsino refuses to accept the report that Olivia does not love him and commands his young intermediary to return to the countess with his suit. Cesario protests that women are capable of great and sincere love and says that his father had a daughter who loved a man as he, *if he were a woman,* might love Orsino. When Orsino inquires further concerning the history of this daughter, Cesario says, "I am all the daughters of my father's house,/And all the brothers too." With this cryptic statement, the page departs to see Olivia.

II,v. Olivia's Garden

Sir Toby, Sir Andrew, and Fabian, each of whom has some pretext for disliking Malvolio, conceal themselves in the box tree as Maria plants her forged letter for the unsuspecting steward. Talking aloud to himself, Malvolio yields to his overweening ambitions and convinces himself that his mistress may be in love with him. While the eavesdroppers whisper derogatory remarks, Malvolio speculates on how he will conduct himself as Olivia's husband. In this mood, he finds Maria's note, which Fabian describes as "A fustian riddle." Misled by self-pride, egotism, and a literal mind, as well as by the clever innuendoes Maria has composed, Malvolio interprets the letter as a declaration of love for him from Olivia. "Some are born great, some achieve greatness, and some have greatness thrust upon 'em," the note reads. The epistle also directs him to be contradictory with Sir Toby and surly with servants, to wear yellow stockings cross-gartered, and to smile at all times. Determined to lose not a moment in complying with these instructions, Malvolio leaves as the tricksters congratulate themselves on the success of their joke. Their elation rises when Maria explains that Olivia has special aversions for all the "singularities" Malvolio has resolved to adopt.

III,i. Olivia's Garden

Cesario, on Orsino's errand to Olivia, meets Feste. After a few moments of banter, he tips the Clown and sends him to his mistress. Feste leaves, and Cesario comments on the skill and insight with which the Clown plies his profession. Sir Toby, accompanied by Sir Andrew, arrives and tells Cesario to go into the house, but before he can do so Olivia and Maria appear. Olivia orders all except Cesario to leave. Again Olivia rejects all pleas on Orsino's behalf and professes her love for Cesario, whom she finds most attractive. Cesario says that he pities Olivia, that he is not what he is (cryptically referring to the masculine disguise), and that no woman has his heart. Olivia pleads with Cesario to return, for his heart may change.

III,ii. Olivia's House

Sir Toby, Sir Andrew, and Fabian are discussing Olivia's apparent fondness for Cesario. Fabian argues that Olivia is really using this device as a means of inciting jealousy in Sir Andrew. Fabian and Sir Toby, foreseeing much amusement, induce Sir Andrew to challenge Cesario to a duel. They promise to deliver the note to Cesario, but after Sir Andrew leaves they agree that neither Sir Andrew nor the youth is likely to force the other to fight. Maria arrives with the news that Malvolio "does obey every point of the letter." He is cross-gartered, in yellow stockings, and "does smile his face into more lines than is in the new map with the augmentation of the Indies."

III,iii. A Street

Out of fondness and concern for Sebastian, Antonio has followed him to the city. Explaining that the Duke and his followers regard him as an enemy, Antonio says that he must keep under cover. He thrusts his purse on Sebastian and arranges to meet him at the Elephant (an inn) in an hour's time.

III,iv. Olivia's House

Eager to have everything in readiness for Cesario's next visit, whenever it may be, Olivia asks Maria the whereabouts of Malvolio. Maria replies that the steward is approaching, that he acts as if he were possessed, and that Olivia should keep some guard near her. Smiling foolishly, Malvolio comes in and converses with Olivia in such odd fashion as to convince her that he is out of his wits. A servant announces the arrival of Cesario. Impatient to see her visitor, Olivia leaves Malvolio in Maria's charge after she directs the waiting woman to place him under the care of the household staff.

Interpreting all that happens as a prearranged plan conforming with the letter he found, Malvolio spurns Maria, Sir Toby, and Fabian, and drives them to increased exasperation and fury. Outraged by their insults, Malvolio leaves his tormentors, and they at once begin plotting to confine the overbearing steward to a madman's cell.

Sir Andrew arrives with a copy of his challenge to Cesario, which Sir Toby reads aloud while Fabian comments on the contents. Having advised Sir Andrew to lie in wait for Cesario and to threaten the page with blustering words and gestures, Sir Toby tells Fabian that he will deliver Sir Andrew's challenge by word of mouth since the ignorance reflected in the written copy would "breed no terror in the youth." The pranksters withdraw as Olivia and Cesario appear. Once again Cesario conveys Orsino's suit and resists Olivia's protestations of love.

Upon Olivia's departure, Sir Toby and Fabian stop Cesario, and Sir Toby informs him of Sir Andrew's violent character and his purpose to precipitate a sword fight. Alarmed and frightened, Cesario beseeches Sir Toby to negotiate with Sir Andrew and to learn what offense the page has committed. Fabian insists that he does not know the cause of Sir Andrew's animosity but offers to make Cesario's peace if he can. They leave, and Sir Toby reappears with Sir Andrew. Sir Toby is describing in vigorous terms the ferocious and bellicose nature of Cesario, and Sir Andrew authorizes Sir Toby to mediate the quarrel, even if he has to give Cesario his horse, "grey Capilet." Fabian and Cesario return, and Sir Toby mischievously persuades each contestant to draw his weapon by assuring him that the other intends no harm.

As Cesario and Sir Andrew draw, Antonio comes on the scene. Mistaking Cesario for Sebastian, the doughty captain intervenes and takes Cesario's place. Sir Toby draws his own sword to oppose Antonio. At this moment, officers appear to arrest the sea captain. Somewhat apologetically, Antonio asks Cesario for his purse or for some of the money in it, but Cesario naturally denies having received it. Saddened and enraged by this apparent ingratitude on the part of the supposed Sebastian, Antonio denounces Cesario, calls him Sebastian, and goes out in custody of the officers.

Antonio's use of the name Sebastian has aroused Viola's interest and curiosity, and she also leaves, hoping against hope that her brother may be alive. Unwilling to miss their fun, Sir Toby and Fabian quickly convince the gullible Sir Andrew that Cesario is a coward, and the three of them set out after the page.

IV,i. In Front of Olivia's House

Feste has mistaken Sebastian for Cesario and is trying to fetch the young man to Olivia's house, but Sebastian refuses to take the Clown seriously and gives him a generous tip. Sir Andrew, Sir Toby, and Fabian discover Sebastian and provoke a quarrel with him, also taking him for Cesario. Feste, realizing the distress of his mistress if Cesario suffers any mishap, scampers off to call her. In the meantime, Sebastian has more than amply repaid Sir Andrew's blow, and Sir Toby involves himself in the struggle in an effort to save Sir Andrew from greater injury. Olivia arrives and supposes that she sees Cesario. She roundly denounces Sir Toby and insists that Sebastian accompany her into the house. Wondering if he is really dreaming, the youth immediately yields to Olivia's request.

IV,ii. Olivia's House

Pressing their practical joke still farther, Maria, Sir Toby, and Feste contrive for the Clown to assume the role of Sir Topas the curate and to converse with Malvolio. The steward speaks from inside a darkened room where he has been confined for treatment of his supposed madness. After pretending to interrogate Malvolio on his sanity, Feste drops the role of Sir Topas and speaks in his own person. Changing from one personality to the other, Feste continues to taunt Malvolio but at last relents and promises to bring him "light and paper and ink." [1]

---

[1] What induces Feste to render this service (pity for the half-crazed steward, fear lest he and his accomplices have carried their prank too far, or some other motive) is a matter each reader of the play must decide for himself.

IV,iii. Olivia's Garden

Alone, Sebastian admires the pearl Olivia has given him and wonders why Antonio did not meet him at the Elephant or if he and Olivia are both mad. Olivia enters with a Priest who has agreed to marry her and Sebastian and to keep their wedding a secret until they wish to celebrate the event publicly. Pledging their loyalty to each other, Olivia and Sebastian follow the Priest into the nearby chantry.

V,i. In Front of Olivia's House

While Feste discourages Fabian from reading Malvolio's letter, Orsino and his attendants arrive. Pleased with Feste's quickness of wit, the Duke rewards the Clown and sends him to fetch Olivia. Officers appear with Antonio, whom Cesario immediately recognizes as the man who rescued him from his scuffle with Sir Andrew. The Duke, however, remembers having seen the man's face in battle. The officers identify Antonio as a public enemy and declare that they have arrested him in a street brawl. Orsino accuses Antonio of piracy and asks what "foolish boldness" has brought him to risk detention. Denying the charge of piracy, Antonio, mistaking Cesario for Sebastian, tells how he saved the young man's life and gave him his purse. Now, he insists, the "most ingrateful boy" will not return his money. Confusion mounts as Orsino and Antonio disagree on where Cesario has been for the preceding three months.

At this instant, Olivia and her attendants arrive. Olivia blames Cesario for breaking an appointment, and Orsino renews his suit of Olivia. Finding Olivia adamant in her rejection of him, Orsino blames Cesario for betraying his trust. Vowing to leave Olivia strictly alone but to exact full revenge on Cesario, the Duke starts to leave. Declaring that he loves Orsino more than he will ever "love wife," Cesario follows him. Olivia, mistaking Cesario for Sebastian, whom she has married, calls for the Priest.

In a few words the Priest testifies that he performed a wedding ceremony between Olivia and her husband only two hours before. Contemptuously, Orsino tells Cesario to keep Olivia but never to meet him again. Cesario starts to protest but is interrupted by Sir Andrew, who rushes in searching for a surgeon for Sir Toby. Sebastian, whom the two knights also mistook for Cesario, has bloodied the heads of both and proved to be "the very devil incardinate." Sir Toby and Feste arrive calling for the surgeon, and Sir Toby supports

Sir Andrew's story. Olivia commands that Sir Toby receive proper care as he leaves with Feste, Fabian, and Sir Andrew.

No sooner are they gone than Sebastian arrives and apologizes to Olivia for having injured Sir Toby. The Duke expresses amazement at the identical appearance of Sebastian and Cesario. Sebastian enthusiastically greets Antonio, who with Olivia shares Orsino's wonder and bewilderment. In a quick exchange of reminiscences Sebastian and Cesario convince each other of their identity and their relationship as brother and sister.

Delighted at the turn of events, Orsino asks for Viola's hand and wishes to see her in "woman's weeds." Viola explains that Malvolio has arranged the imprisonment of the Sea Captain with whom she left her feminine apparel. In order to effect the Captain's release, Olivia sends for Malvolio and then remembers that reports say "he's much distract." Seeing Feste and Fabian, Olivia asks the Clown about Malvolio. In reply Feste offers Malvolio's letter to his mistress, who orders the Clown to read it. The irrepressible Feste begins reading in a loud and unnatural voice, and Olivia commands Fabian to read in the Clown's place. In a brief summary, Malvolio charges Olivia with abuse and maintains his sanity. Upon hearing the letter, Olivia orders Fabian to bring Malvolio to her. She then suggests that Orsino and she celebrate their weddings with one feast, for which she will bear the cost. Orsino gladly accepts and pledges his troth to Viola.

Fabian leads in Malvolio, who accuses Olivia of having done him "Notorious wrong" and asks her to explain the chain of coincidences that misled him into the foolish actions resulting in his confinement for madness. Olivia identifies the handwriting of the prankish note as Maria's and begins to reconstruct the practical joke. She promises Malvolio that "when we know the grounds and authors of it" he will be "both the plaintiff and the judge" of his own cause.

Recalling the remarkable events of the present hour, Fabian confesses his own and Sir Toby's roles in their revenge on Malvolio. He also recounts how Sir Toby persuaded Maria to write the letter and has married her "In recompense." Olivia expresses pity for Malvolio, but Feste yields to a final opportunity to taunt the steward and to boast of his own part in the extended prank. Exclaiming "I'll be reveng'd on the whole pack of you!" Malvolio rushes out. Olivia admits the cruelty of the joke, and Orsino orders that peace be made with the steward, who still possesses testimony regarding the Sea Captain. The couples and their attendants depart for the coming feast, leaving Feste to sing a concluding lyric.

TROILUS AND CRESSIDA [1] [1601–1602]

CHARACTERS

PRIAM, King of Troy.

HECTOR,
TROILUS,
PARIS, } his sons.
DEIPHOBUS,
HELENUS [a Priest],

MARGARELON, a bastard son of *Priam*.

AENEAS, } Trojan commanders.
ANTENOR,

CALCHAS, a Trojan priest, taking part with the Greeks.

PANDARUS, uncle to *Cressida*.

AGAMEMNON, the Greek general.

MENELAUS, his brother.

ACHILLES,
AJAX,
ULYSSES, } Greek commanders.
NESTOR,
DIOMEDES,
PATROCLUS,

THERSITES, a deformed and scurrilous Greek.

ALEXANDER, servant to *Cressida*.

Servant to *Troilus*.

Servant to *Paris*.

Servant to *Diomedes*.

HELEN, wife to *Menelaus*.

ANDROMACHE, wife to *Hector*.

CASSANDRA, daughter to *Priam*, a prophetess.

CRESSIDA, daughter to *Calchas*.

Trojan and Greek Soldiers, and Attendants.

Scene: *Troy, and the Greek Camp in front of it*

Prologue

The Prologue, in armor, briefly recounts how sixty-nine Greek princes sailed from Athens to ransack Troy, where Paris sleeps with

[1] Although scholars have differed in their classification of this play, the majority of critics today regard it as a comedy.

Helen, Menelaus's queen. The war has gone on for several years.

I,i. Troy. In Front of Priam's Palace

Troilus, infatuated with Cressida and discouraged at the slow progress of his affair with her, tells Pandarus that he is weary of fighting the Greeks and will have no more of it. Pandarus, who has served as go-between for the two lovers, pleads with Troilus to exercise patience but tires of his laments, says that Cressida is a fool not to join her father Calchas in the Greek camp, and vows to meddle no more in the matter. He leaves, and Troilus reflects that Helen is an unworthy object to fight for. While Troilus wonders how he can regain the assistance of Pandarus, Aeneas appears and persuades Troilus to accompany him to the battlefield.

I,ii. Troy. A Street

Alexander explains to Cressida that people are on their way to watch the struggle between the Greek and Trojan champions. Pandarus joins them and in bantering fashion praises Troilus above Hector and Paris. While they are talking, Aeneas, Antenor, Hector, Paris, Helenus, and Troilus file past on their way from the battleground to Troy. As they go, Pandarus suggests that Troilus is superior to each of the others. A crowd of common soldiers marches by, but Pandarus scorns them as "Asses, fools, dolts! chaff and bran." He even scoffs at Cressida's notion that Achilles is a better man than Troilus. Troilus's servant summons Pandarus, who promises to bring Cressida a token from her sweetheart and leaves. In a short soliloquy, Cressida states that she finds more virtues in Troilus than Pandarus has praised. She then explains why she will continue to keep Troilus at arm's length in order to whet his desire for her.

I,iii. The Greek Camp. In Front of Agamemnon's Tent

Agamemnon and his fellow commanders are reviewing the sober fact that after a siege of seven years the walls of Troy still stand. Agamemnon attributes the impasse to Jove, who would test the constancy of men with long trials; Nestor explains the deadlock as a means of identifying men of true courage who overcome chance and master misfortune; Ulysses ascribes the stalemate to disorganization among the Greeks and to their inability to maintain proper degree and order among themselves.

Ulysses goes on to describe how Achilles and Patroclus keep to their tent and idly amuse themselves by impersonating and mocking their fellow officers. Nestor adds that Ajax, seeking to emulate Achilles and Patroclus, rails against the war and baits Thersites into making abusive and discrediting comments about the Greeks. All the while the malcontents accuse the other leaders of cowardice and make light of prudence and farsightedness.

At the height of this conference Aeneas arrives bearing Hector's open challenge to fight any Greek champion on the following day. Agamemnon and Nestor both promise to meet Hector if no younger warrior volunteers. While the other Greeks escort Aeneas to a feast in Agamemnon's tent, Nestor and Ulysses discuss Hector's challenge, which they correctly interpret as aimed at Achilles. Nestor, judging that Achilles is the only Greek who stands any chance in combat against Hector, thinks it appropriate that the two champions engage each other. Ulysses, however, advises against such a course: (1) if Achilles wins, his pride and insolence will make him even more insufferable; (2) if Hector wins, the Greeks will lose status through the defeat of their strongest warrior. For these reasons Ulysses proposes that through a predetermined casting of lots they designate the stupid Ajax to oppose Hector. By praising Ajax as the worthier man, the Greeks may punish Achilles and cure him of his vanity. Pleased, Nestor departs to advise Agamemnon of the scheme.

II,i. The Greek Camp

Ajax demands that Thersites explain the proclamation of Hector's challenge. Thersites answers him with insults, and the two men trade scurrilous epithets with each other. Frequently Ajax strikes his tormentor, but Thersites rails more loudly. Achilles and Patroclus approach and try to learn the cause of the quarrel. Thersites caustically describes Ajax as a fool whose "pia mater is not worth the ninth part of a sparrow" and says that he "wears his wit in his belly and his guts in his head." He adds that Ulysses and Nestor have yoked Achilles and Ajax like "draught oxen" and make them "plough up the wars." Patroclus tries to calm Thersites, who promptly labels Patroclus Achilles's brach (hound bitch) and departs. Achilles interprets Hector's challenge for Ajax's benefit, terms it "trash," and says that a lottery will determine the Greek contender. Ajax goes to learn more about the business.

II,ii. Troy. Priam's Palace

Priam has received a proposal from Nestor that the Trojans return Helen and thus end the war; he now seeks the advice of his sons. Hector, calm and of proved courage, says that Helen is not worth a fraction of the bloodshed she has caused and favors surrendering her. Troilus strongly objects to this plan on the grounds that manhood and honor outweigh reason and practicality. In the ensuing argument Helenus sides with Hector; Paris says nothing; Troilus insists that the Trojans applauded Paris when he captured Helen and that they should not now be afraid to keep the prize. In the midst of the discussion, Cassandra walks past, raving and prophesying the destruction of Troy unless they let Helen go. Hector inquires if her "high strains/Of divination" give Troilus pause, but Troilus regards Cassandra as mad and refuses to pay any attention to her "brain-sick raptures." Paris observes that if he had the power to assume all the difficulties of the conflict on himself he would not retract what he has done. Priam accuses Paris of having a selfish spirit, but Paris insists that giving Helen back to the Greeks would disgrace all Trojans and dishonor Helen herself. Hector reminds the others that Helen is wife to Sparta's king and that the "moral laws/Of nature and of nations speak aloud/To have her back return'd." Nevertheless, Troilus and Paris have argued persuasively, and Hector casts his vote with theirs to keep Helen. Troilus declares that the glory and renown of combat rather than the defense of Helen justify continuing the war, and Hector tells of the challenge that he hopes will goad Achilles into action.

II,iii. The Greek Camp. In Front of the Tent of Achilles

In an abusive soliloquy, Thersites predicts that if Troy is not captured until Ajax and Achilles undermine it "the walls will stand till they fall of themselves." Thersites calls for Achilles and reviles Patroclus, who replies in kind. Achilles appears, and Thersites continues his scurrilous raillery until Agamemnon approaches with his fellow commanders. Achilles tells Patroclus that he will speak with nobody and retires into his tent. Thersites, observing that the war is based on a whore and a cuckold, follows Achilles.

Ajax declares that Achilles is suffering from pride, and Agamemnon sends Patroclus on a series of messages to Achilles in a vain attempt to induce the champion to emerge from his tent. Tired of using Patroclus as an intermediary, Agamemnon delegates Ulysses to fetch

Achilles forth. During Ulysses's absence, Agamemnon grossly flatters Ajax on his strength, wisdom, nobility, and superiority to Achilles. Ulysses proves unsuccessful in moving Achilles, and Agamemnon suggests that they send Ajax on the same mission. Ulysses hastens to veto this plan in a speech shrewdly calculated to flatter Ajax and build up his self-pride. While Ajax boasts of how he will chasten Achilles with brute force, the other commanders subtly inspire his self-confidence and appoint him to meet Hector on the morrow.

III,i. Troy. Priam's Palace

To the accompaniment of music, Pandarus asks the servant to call Paris, for whom Pandarus has a message from Troilus. Paris and Helen enter with their attendants and engage Pandarus in a gay and somewhat bawdy conversation which refers to Troilus and Cressida and leads Pandarus to render a love song as compensation for the music he has interrupted. Infatuated with Helen, Paris has not joined in the day's battle; nor has Troilus, who is sulking. Pandarus leaves. Paris and Helen go to greet the warriors as they return from battle.

III,ii. Troy. The Orchard of Pandarus

Dismissing his servant, Troilus pleads with Pandarus to accompany him to Cressida's house. Pandarus tells Troilus to wait in the orchard and Cressida will come to him. After whetting Troilus's anticipation with a brief description of Cressida's excitement at meeting him, Pandarus brings his niece, teases the two lovers, and leaves them. Cressida feigns coyness until Pandarus returns and chides the couple for too much talking. She then admits that she pretended to be hard to woo and professes her love for Troilus. Cressida invites a kiss, but immediately claims that she is ashamed of her forwardness. At last the lovers pledge everlasting loyalty to each other. Pandarus delightedly witnesses the bargain and volunteers to escort them to a room with a bed.

III,iii. The Greek Camp

Calchas begs the Greeks to reward his faithful service by exchanging the Trojan prisoner Antenor for Cressida. Agamemnon orders Diomedes to supervise the negotiations and to inform Hector that Ajax is ready to answer the challenge.

After Diomedes and Calchas have departed, Ulysses notices that Achilles and Patroclus are lounging in the entrance of their tent.

He suggests that the Greek commanders file past, paying no attention to the idle champions. Ulysses suspects that Achilles will question him, and he has "derision med'cinable" ready.

Puzzled and offended by the treatment of the generals who stroll by, Achilles asks Ulysses what he is reading. Seizing the opportunity, Ulysses praises Ajax and says that the Greek lords are already applauding his exploits and victory over Hector and Troy. Achilles inquires if his own deeds have been forgotten, and Ulysses reminds him that perseverance alone keeps honor bright and that good deeds past are "forgot as soon/As done." Virtue must not, Ulysses says, "seek/Remuneration for the thing it was!" Achilles should not wonder at Ajax's present popularity "Since things in motion sooner catch the eye/Than what not stirs."

Achilles says that he has strong reasons for maintaining his privacy, and Ulysses tells him that his love for Polyxena, daughter of Priam, is well-known. Taunting Achilles for yielding to Hector's sister whereas Ajax defeats Hector, Ulysses leaves. Patroclus blames himself for having distracted Achilles from heroic deeds, and at last Achilles perceives that his reputation is at stake and his fame imperiled. He asks Patroclus to call Thersites to serve as an emissary to Ajax.

Before Patroclus can go, however, Thersites appears and describes the strutting vanity of Ajax, who is daydreaming in anticipation of his combat with Hector. Achilles and Patroclus direct Thersites to request Ajax to arrange for Hector to visit Achilles under a truce guaranteeing him safe-conduct.

IV,i. Troy. A Street

Aeneas and his servant meet Paris, Deiphobus, Antenor, Diomedes, and others at night. Paris tells Aeneas that they have come to effect the exchange of Antenor for Cressida. Paris, supposing that Troilus is at Cressida's house, asks Aeneas to precede them and warn Troilus of the party's approach. Aeneas leaves with his servant, and Paris asks Diomedes, "Who in your thoughts deserves fair Helen best/Myself or Menelaus?" Cynically Diomedes says that their claims are equal, for Menelaus "like a puling cuckold" would gladly accept what other men have cast aside, and Paris would "out of whorish loins" breed his heirs. Diomedes adds that a Greek has died for every drop of blood in Helen's "bawdy veins" and a Trojan has perished for every dram of her "contaminated carrion weight."

IV,ii. Troy. The Court of Pandarus's House

Troilus and Cressida are bidding farewell after a night of love-making. Pandarus discovers them and teases them about their affair. A knocking interrupts their conversation; Troilus and Cressida depart; Aeneas enters and asks for Troilus. While Pandarus is denying knowledge of Troilus's whereabouts, Troilus returns. Aeneas informs Troilus that arrangements are complete to deliver Cressida into the custody of Diomedes. Requesting that Aeneas not reveal where he has found him, Troilus accompanies Aeneas to meet the group arranging the exchange.

Cressida comes back and learns from Pandarus that she must go over to the Greek camp. Vowing that she will never leave Troy or Troilus, she goes into the house to bewail her fate.

IV,iii. Troy. A Street in Front of Pandarus's House

On Paris's urging, Troilus promises to bring Cressida immediately and deliver her to Diomedes. He departs, and Paris wishes he "could help" his brother.

IV,iv. Troy. Pandarus's House

While Cressida is telling Pandarus that she cannot be moderate in her grief, Troilus enters and tells her that the gods have separated them because they envy the purity of his love. She asks if it is true that she must leave him; he assures her that it is and that she must go at once. Pandarus departs. Troilus and Cressida repeatedly affirm their loyalty to each other and exchange a sleeve and glove as favors. Troilus says that he will bribe the Greek sentinels to let him visit her every night, and he cautions her against the wiles and romantic talents of the Grecian youths. Aeneas and Paris have been calling to them, and Troilus at last tells Paris to bring Aeneas and Diomedes into the room. Welcoming Diomedes, Troilus warns him to treat Cressida courteously and threatens him if he does not. Haughtily, Diomedes replies that he will prize her according to her worth but not because Troilus commands him to value her. Troilus, Diomedes, and Cressida leave together as the others hear Hector's trumpet and prepare to witness his combat with Ajax.

IV,v. The Greek Camp. Lists Set Out

Ajax, armed for battle, arrives on the field with his fellow Greek commanders. On Agamemnon's encouragement, Ajax blows his trumpet. While they wait for a reply, Diomedes and Cressida approach them. Several of the Greek generals welcome Cressida and kiss her in turn while she jests with them. Diomedes finally takes her to meet her father, and Ulysses describes her to Nestor as a wanton and provocative flirt.

On the arrival of Hector and his escort, Aeneas and Agamemnon discuss the conditions of the coming conflict. Agamemnon delegates Aeneas and Diomedes to act as judges. While Ajax and Hector prepare for combat, Ulysses describes Troilus as Hector's equal and the "second hope" of Troy. Because Hector and Ajax are first cousins, Hector does not elect to renew the struggle after their first trial of strength. The kinsmen embrace, and Hector and Troilus accept the Grecians' invitation to dinner.

With chivalrous courtesy, Hector and his hosts exchange greetings. Hector and Ulysses start to argue the outcome of the war, but Hector observes that Time, "that old common arbitrator . . ./Will one day end it." Ulysses agrees, and Achilles interrupts to boast of how he will slay Hector. With dignity Hector rebukes Achilles for his insolence and goads him into accepting a trial by combat the following day. Friends for the evening, they start for Agamemnon's tent. Lingering behind the others, Troilus induces Ulysses to guide him to Menelaus's tent, where Calchas, Diomedes, and Cressida are feasting. In reply to the Greek's question, Troilus says that Cressida loved and was beloved in Troy, but he does not identify himself as her lover.

V,i. The Greek Camp. In Front of the Tent of Achilles

Achilles tells Patroclus that he will warm Hector's blood with wine this night and cool it with his scimitar on the morrow. Thersites, characteristically obscene, brings a letter to Achilles. While Achilles is reading the missive, Thersites calls Patroclus Achilles's "masculine whore" and further reviles him. Achilles reveals that he has received a letter from Queen Hecuba and a token from Polyxena reminding him of his sworn oath. Consequently he is "thwarted quite" from his great purpose in the next day's battle with Hector. He and Patroclus depart to prepare for the evening's revelry. Thersites soliloquizes on the rashness of Achilles and Patroclus, on the stupidity and loose living of Agamemnon, and on the cuckoldry of Menelaus, declaring that he would rather be any miserable beast or creature than Menelaus.

Hector, Troilus, and their Greek hosts enter with lights. After bidding one another good night, they separate, Troilus and Ulysses following Diomedes toward the tent of Calchas. Hector, Ajax, and Nestor accompany Achilles to his tent. Thersites expresses his distrust of Diomedes, whom he suspects of keeping a Trojan prostitute in Calchas's tent. Cynically, Thersites says that "Nothing but lechery" exists.

V,ii. The Greek Camp. In Front of the Tent of Calchas

While Troilus and Ulysses watch and listen at a distance, Calchas sends Cressida out to meet Diomedes. Thersites has followed Troilus and Ulysses and interjects lewd interpretations of the ensuing scene. As Troilus listens to Diomedes and Cressida, he realizes that the Greek has seduced Cressida and that she has proved false to her pledge of loyalty. Cressida leaves Diomedes for a moment and returns with the sleeve that Troilus gave her as a reminder of their love. With feigned reluctance, she gives it to Diomedes and promises to keep a tryst with him the following night. Diomedes leaves her, and Cressida reflects briefly on her dilemma in changing lovers.

Bewildered, disillusioned, and frustrated, but convinced of Cressida's infidelity to him, Troilus vows to Ulysses that he will split Diomedes's helmet, on which the Greek has said he will wear the sleeve Cressida has given him. Aeneas comes to escort Troilus home, and Thersites again descants on the popularity of wars and lechery.

V,iii. Troy. In Front of Priam's Palace

Andromache begs Hector not to fight this day, because her dreams are ominous. Cassandra enters and adds her voice to Andromache's, but Hector remains determined, saying that honor is "far more precious-dear than life." Troilus, armed and ready for combat, joins Hector and chides him for having oftentimes proved too merciful and lenient to his enemies. Hector forbids Troilus to accompany him, but Troilus declares that no one can hinder him in his fierce purpose. At Cassandra's urging, Priam tries to deter Hector, but the King at last yields to his son's insistence and invokes the blessing of the gods upon him. All depart except Troilus, to whom Pandarus brings a letter. To his friend's inquiry about the contents, Troilus says that the letter contains "mere words." He tears it into pieces and adds, "My love with words and errors still she feeds,/But edifies another with her deeds."

V,iv. The Field between Troy and the Greek Camp

Thersites continues his cynical commentary. Diomedes and Troilus are battling over a whore; the subtle scheming of Ulysses and Nestor has proved futile; Ajax is showing himself to be prouder than Achilles was. Diomedes and Troilus pass by, fighting with each other. Hector discovers Thersites but spares him, and Thersites follows Diomedes and Troilus.

V,v. Another Part of the Field

Diomedes directs his servant to take Troilus's horse to Cressida with word that he has "chastis'd the amorous Trojan." Agamemnon appears, listing the Greek casualties. Nestor follows him with orders to convey the body of Patroclus to Achilles. Ulysses comes with word that Achilles has roused the Myrmidons to avenge the death of Patroclus and that Ajax "foams at the mouth." Ajax passes, shouting after Troilus, and Achilles is searching for Hector.

V,vi. Another Part of the Field

Troilus attacks Ajax and Diomedes together. Achilles and Hector exchange taunts. Troilus dashes up with news that Ajax has captured Aeneas and rushes away to rescue him. Hector spies a Greek in armor and pursues him.

V,vii. Another Part of the Field

Achilles instructs his Myrmidons on how they are to ambush Hector and kill him. Paris and Menelaus are fighting with each other. Margarelon accosts Thersites. When Margarelon identifies himself as "A bastard son of Priam's," Thersites says that he too is a bastard and that two bastards should not quarrel with each other.

V,viii. Another Part of the Field

Hector, exhausted, disarms in order to rest. Achilles, ignoring his appeal for fair play, commands the Myrmidons to slay him. Then he orders his men to tie the Trojan champion's body to his horse's tail so that he may drag it triumphantly about the field.

V,ix. Another Part of the Field

Agamemnon and his fellow commanders hear the shouts accompanying Hector's death and realize that Troy has fallen and the "sharp wars are ended."

V,x. Another Part of the Field

Troilus informs Aeneas, Paris, Antenor, and Deiphobus of Hector's death and of the abuse to his corpse. Pessimistically aware of the effect this action will have in Troy, Troilus vows to haunt Achilles and gain revenge. Pandarus appears and calls to Troilus, who curtly tells him to pursue his life with shame and ignominy and to live forever with his name. Left to himself, Pandarus laments the fact that he has suffered the usual end of bawds and go-betweens.

ALL'S WELL THAT ENDS WELL
[1602–1604]

CHARACTERS

THE KING OF FRANCE.

THE DUKE OF FLORENCE.

BERTRAM, COUNT OF ROSSIL-
LION.

LAFEW, an old lord.

PAROLLES, a follower of *Bertram*.

Two French Lords, with *Bertram*.

RYNALDO, steward to the *Countess*.

LAVATCH, a clown, servant to the
Countess.

A Page.

COUNTESS OF ROSSILLION,
mother to *Bertram*.

HELENA [daughter of Gerard de
Narbon], a gentlewoman, pro-
tected by the *Countess*.

A Widow of Florence.

DIANA [*Capilet*], her daughter.

VIOLENTA,[1] neighbors and
MARIANA, friends to the
Widow.

Lords, Soldiers, etc.

Scene: *Rossillion;*[2] *Paris; Florence; Marseilles*

I,i. Rossillion. The Count's Palace

Bertram is taking leave of his widowed mother to place himself
under the guardianship of the King of France, whom Lafew describes
as virtuous and generous but suffering from an abscess that his physicians have pronounced incurable. The Countess introduces her
ward Helena as the daughter of a famous practitioner who, if he were
living, could cure the King's ailment. While the Countess praises
Helena's father and the girl's own character, Helena begins to weep.
Giving Bertram her blessing, the Countess retires. Bertram and
Lafew take farewell of Helena. Temporarily alone, Helena confesses

[1] Some editors omit Violenta from the list of characters.
[2] Editions vary in their spelling of this proper noun.

that she sheds tears for the departing Bertram, with whom she is deeply in love, rather than for the reasons the Countess and Lafew have supposed. As Parolles approaches, Helena describes him as a friend of Bertram but "a notorious liar," fool, and coward. After a cynical commentary on virginity, Parolles goes to overtake Bertram. Briefly Helena speculates that people must plan their actions rather than depend on fate or providence. She intimates that she is thinking of some project relating to the King's disease.

I,ii. Paris. The King's Palace

Receiving reports on the war between Florence and Siena, the King decrees that the French gentlemen, eager for military service, may enlist on either side. On the arrival of Bertram, Lafew, and Parolles, the King extends Bertram a hearty welcome. Bertram's resemblance to his father reminds the King of the former Count of Rossillion, whose character and wisdom he eulogizes extravagantly. Ill and discouraged, the King desires that he, like Bertram's father, might die and escape a useless and unprofitable life. Having heard of the healing skill of Helena's father and exhausted by the "applications" of his court physicians, the monarch inquires about Gerard de Narbon and wishes that he were yet alive.

I,iii. Rossillion. The Count's Palace

Rynaldo is starting to reveal news of Helena to the Countess, but Lavatch interrupts to gain his mistress's permission to leave her service and marry Isbel. Wearying of the Clown's half-humorous, half-bawdy pleading, the Countess dismisses him. At once Rynaldo tells the Countess that he has overheard Helena confessing to herself her love for Bertram. Commending Rynaldo for his honesty and admitting that his report does not completely astonish her, she sends the steward out as Helena enters.

Professing her affection for Helena, the Countess describes their relationship as that of mother and daughter. Helena protests that Bertram cannot be her brother because of differences in their rank and family status. Seeing Helena's growing confusion and embarrassment, the Countess orders the girl to declare whether she loves Bertram or not. With numerous apologies, Helena admits that she loves Bertram and has been planning to go to Paris. Although hope of seeing Bertram is her chief purpose, she is willing to stake her life that she can cure the King with prescriptions she has inherited from her father. The Countess graciously approves Helena's journey, offers assistance, and says that she will pray God's blessing on her trip.

II,i. Paris. The King's Palace

Various young lords are preparing to enlist in the Florentine War. Admonishing them to gallant and honorable conduct, the ailing King retires. Bertram is chafing because he has not won permission to accompany this expedition, and Parolles boasts of his own former exploits in battle against the Spinii. As Bertram and Parolles depart to "take a more dilated farewell" of their companions, the King returns. Then Lafew seeks and secures permission to introduce Helena, ushers her in, and leaves her and the King together.

Identifying herself as the daughter of the late Gerard de Narbon, Helena expresses confidence that she can cure the King. Skeptical of submitting himself to further treatment, the King at first declines her services but finally yields in the face of her willingness to accept death as a punishment if she fails. If she succeeds in helping him, the King promises to wed her to the man of her choice.

II,ii. Rossillion. The Count's Palace

Following a merry conversation with Lavatch, the Countess sends the Clown to court with a message for Helena. She requests an immediate answer.

II,iii. The King's Palace

While Lafew, Parolles, and Bertram talk about the miraculous recovery of the King, the monarch enters with Helena and attendants. Summoning all the lords in court, the King invites Helena to indicate the one whom she desires for a husband. Rejecting one after another, Helena at last offers herself and her service to Bertram, saying, "This is the man." Pleading that he may use his own judgment in marriage, Bertram argues that he would be shamed to wed a "poor physician's daughter." Rebuking him for his false pride, the King tells him that Helena possesses all desirable virtues and is to honor born; furthermore, as king he can elevate her to the peerage.

"I cannot love her, nor will strive to do't," Bertram declares, and Helena urges the King to rescind his request. Determined to fulfill his promise to Helena, however, the King commands Bertram to take Helena by the hand and orders that the ceremony take place that night. When the others have gone, Parolles and Lafew start a discussion of what has taken place but quarrel as Parolles grows boastful and insolent to the old lord. Lafew departs briefly and returns with the news that the wedding has been celebrated.

Bertram then finds Parolles and states his intention of leaving for the Florentine War without consummating his marriage. He will send Helena to the Countess with a letter expressing his hate for his new bride and explaining his departure. He will also write the King what he "durst not speak."

II,iv. Paris. The King's Palace

Lavatch is transmitting the Countess's greetings to Helena. Parolles enters and after quibbling with Lavatch, tells Helena that Bertram is leaving on business and desires Helena to depart from court and attend his further pleasure.

II,v. Paris. The King's Palace

Lafew expresses his distrust of Parolles but asks Bertram to act as mediator in their quarrel. Bertram's half-hearted and unsuccessful effort to reconcile Parolles and Lafew results only in Lafew's repeated description of Parolles as an untrustworthy fool.

Bertram and his friend dismiss the departing Lafew for "an idle Lord," as Helena appears. Bertram, pleading urgent business, gives Helena a letter to deliver to the Countess. Ignoring Helena's hint that he should kiss her good-by, Bertram dismisses his wife and leaves with Parolles.

III,i. Florence. The Duke's Palace

Unable to understand why the King of France has not given more positive support to the Florentine War, the Duke welcomes the French lords who have joined him and promises them suitable reward for their services.

III,ii. Rossillion. The Count's Palace

Lavatch brings the Countess a letter from Bertram and leaves. In the note Bertram tells his mother that he is sending her Helena, whom he has wedded, "not bedded," and that he has "sworn to make the 'not' eternal." For this reason he is running away. The Countess voices her condemnation of Bertram's actions as Lavatch returns to announce the arrival of Helena and two gentlemen escorting her. One of the gentlemen reports that Bertram has entered the service of the Duke of Florence. Helen reads the Countess another letter from Bertram in which he declares that until Helena can procure the ring off his finger and show him a child of whom he is the father she must never call him husband.

In the presence of Helena and the two gentlemen, the Countess disowns Bertram and says that the only thing too good for him in France is Helena. Deploring the fact that Bertram has selected Parolles for a companion, the Countess instructs the gentlemen to tell Bertram that he has lost more honor than his sword can ever win in battle. Taking these messengers with her, she goes out to write a letter to her son. In a soliloquy, Helena blames herself for driving Bertram from home into the dangers of war. She vows that if he returns safely she will be gone from Rossillion.

III,iii. Florence. In Front of the Duke's Palace

Bertram declares to the Duke that he will prove himself worthy of his promotion to General of the Horse.

III,iv. Rossillion. The Count's Palace

Rynaldo rereads to the Countess a letter from Helena in which the unhappy girl has declared her intention of leaving Rossillion, becoming a pilgrim, and freeing Bertram from his marriage bonds. The Countess upbraids Rynaldo for not having anticipated Helena's flight when she handed him the letter and for not enabling the Countess to forestall her departure. Unable to decide whether Bertram or Helena is dearer to her, the Countess commands Rynaldo to write Bertram the news in the hope that he and Helena may both return to Rossillion.

III,v. Outside the Walls of Florence

As the battle moves from their range of vision, the Widow cautions Diana against the possible advances of Bertram, and Mariana adds her warning against Parolles, who has already made improper proposals to Diana and has seduced many maidens. Helena, disguised as a pilgrim, appears and seeks lodging in the Widow's house. Welcoming Helena as a guest and recognizing that she is French, the Widow and Diana tell her of the valor of Count Rossillion who, according to rumor, has come from France to escape his forced marriage. Helena admits that she has heard of Bertram but denies knowing him, although she says that she is acquainted with his wife. Diana comments that Parolles has described Bertram's wife as a coarse person. When Helena agrees and says the lady's only virtue is "a reserved honesty," the Widow observes that Diana could do the wife a good turn inasmuch as Bertram has solicited Diana for her favors. As Bertram and Parolles lead their troops past, Helena pretends not to recognize either one. Diana praises Bertram's handsomeness and wishes that he were more chaste in character; she also blames Parolles for introducing Bertram to brothels. After the army has passed, Helena invites the Widow and her companions to supper.

III,vi. Camp in Front of Florence

Attempting to convince Bertram of Parolles's cowardice, two French lords persuade the Count to test him by permitting him to recapture the drum he has lost in the preceding battle. One of the lords will feign an attack, capture Parolles, and trick him into betraying Bertram, who will secretly witness the business. Parolles appears, and Bertram goads him into vowing that he will recapture the drum. Parolles leaves, and the two lords assure Bertram that they will expose the real and cowardly character of his comrade. After one of the lords departs, Bertram offers to introduce the other to Diana, "a fair creature."

III,vii. Florence. The Widow's House

Having convinced the Widow that she is actually Bertram's wife and having given her a purse of gold with the promise of additional reward, Helena persuades her to permit her daughter to make an assignation with Bertram. Diana is also to demand Bertram's ring as a pledge of his intention to keep the appointment. Helena will then impersonate Diana and keep the tryst. Afterward Helena will given Diana three thousand crowns as a marriage portion. The Widow consents, and they decide to carry out their plot that very night.

IV,i. Near the Florentine Camp

One of the French lords and five or six soldiers hide themselves as Parolles approaches talking to himself. Afraid to attempt the recovery of the drum, an act he knows to be impossible, Parolles reviews the practicality of wounding himself or of tearing his clothes and breaking his sword in order to convince his friends that he has incurred great danger in his exploit. Suddenly the French lord and soldiers seize Parolles and blindfold him. Immediately he offers to tell them all the military secrets he knows to save his life. The lord places Parolles under guard and sends for Bertram.

IV,ii. Florence. The Widow's House

Manifesting coldness to Bertram's advances, Diana succeeds in wheedling the ring from him. She then instructs him to come to her window at midnight and to remain speechless with her for an hour after their love-making and says that she will place another ring on his finger. Bertram, impassioned in his anticipation of their tryst, leaves her, and Diana reflects that she is innocent of any sin in her deception.

IV,iii. The Florentine Camp

While waiting with their soldiers for Bertram to appear, the two French lords talk about various rumors they have heard. They criticize Bertram for having deserted Helena and for seducing Diana. They have also learned that Bertram knows of Helena's pilgrimage and the rumors of her death. The Florentine War has ended, and they speculate on what Bertram will do. A messenger comes with news that Bertram has taken his leave of the Duke, has received letters of commendation from him, and plans to return to France in the morning.

After midnight Bertram joins the lords. He states that he has made his arrangements to leave Florence, has buried a wife and mourned for her, has written his mother of his plan to return, and has "effected many nicer needs." He is ready to confront Parolles, who has been in stocks and signed a confession to a supposed friar called Morgan. In the interview that follows, Parolles betrays strategic military information to his supposed captors and slanders the reputations of many of his fellow officers. Bertram's disillusionment is complete when the Interpreter reads Parolles's letter to Diana warning her against "the allurement of one Count Rossillion, a foolish idle boy . . . very ruttish." After Parolles consents to betray the Duke of Florence and Bertram into their enemies' hands, Bertram and his companions remove the braggart's blindfold and identify themselves. Taunting him, they depart. Parolles consoles himself with the thought that although he will never again be a captain he "will eat, and drink, and sleep as soft/As captain shall," and he concludes that "There's place and means for every man alive."

IV,iv. Florence. The Widow's House

Confident of the King's gratitude for his recovery, Helena prepares to conduct the Widow and Diana to Marseilles, where she will seek royal permission to return to Rossillion. She reminds the Widow of her reported death and promises to assist in arranging a desirable marriage for Diana. She exhorts them to make haste and assures them that "All's well that ends well."

IV,v. Rossillion. The Count's Palace

Lafew and the Countess are discussing the rascality of Parolles, whom they blame for the waywardness of Bertram and the death of Helena. Lavatch engages Lafew in a series of bawdy jests until Lafew tires of the Clown and dismisses him. The Countess agrees that Lavatch is a rascal but explains that he has got out of hand because the deceased Count promised him lifelong security in the household. Lafew tells the Countess that, in light of Helena's death, the King has approved the betrothal of Bertram and Lafew's daughter. To this match the Countess gives her blessing and invites Lafew to remain at Rossillion until the arrival of Bertram and the King. Latvatch re-enters to announce the coming of Bertram and his escort.

V,i. Marseilles. A Street

Helena, the Widow, and Diana, with attendants, wearily make their way through the city. Recognizing a gentleman as a member of the French court, Helena asks him to present her petition for an audience to the King. The gentleman tells her that the King has already left Marseilles on his way to Rossillion. He agrees to convey Helena's paper to the monarch, and Helena plans to follow without delay.

V,ii. Rossillion. The Count's Palace

Lavatch refuses to deliver Parolles's letter to Lafew, who enters as the Clown scurrilously characterizes Parolles and departs. Lafew turns a deaf ear to Parolles's appeal for assistance, gives the rascal a small tip, and taunts him with the episode of the drum. Relenting somewhat, Lafew says, "Though you are a fool and a knave, you shall eat."

V,iii. Rossillion. The Count's Palace

Continuing to grieve for Helena, the King yields to the Countess's entreaties and says that he has "forgiven and forgotten all" of Bertram's offenses. Lafew tells the King that Bertram has agreed to the new marriage. Bertram enters, submits to his betrothal to

Lafew's daughter, and says that after Helena's death he has discovered that he loved her.

In the midst of this rejoicing Lafew asks Bertram to give him a favor for his fiancée. When Bertram hands him a ring, Lafew recognizes it as similar to one Helena was wearing when she left the French court. Bertram denies that the ring belonged to Helena, but the King examines it and identifies it as one he, himself, gave Helena. Although the King, the Countess, and Lafew testify that the ring is Helena's, Bertram persists that they are all mistaken and that he obtained the ring from a Florentine lady. Convinced that Bertram is lying and suspicious that he has abused Helena, the King orders his arrest. Bertram defiantly says that if any person proves the ring to be Helena's, he could just as easily prove that he, Bertram, consummated his marriage with her. He then departs under guard.

While the King is "wrapp'd in dismal thinkings," the gentleman enters with Helena's letter in which she signs herself Diana Capilet and beseeches the King to wed her to Bertram, who has seduced her. Lafew rejects Bertram as a potential son-in-law. The King, persuaded that Helena has been the victim of foul play, orders his attendants to bring Bertram back and to admit the petitioners.

After the Widow and Diana introduce themselves, the King asks Bertram for his explanation. In the face of Diana's accusations, Bertram tries to shrug her off as a common prostitute. Diana, however, shows the valuable ring Bertram gave her, and the Countess identifies it as an heirloom "Conferr'd by testament to th' sequent issue" of the Rossillion family. Diana suggests that Parolles, unworthy as he is, could testify in the matter, and the King sends for him.

As the evidence against him mounts, Bertram confesses that he has had an affair with Diana and pleads that his youthful passion led him to pay the outrageous price she demanded. Diana then says that she will return the ring to Bertram if he will give back her own ring, which the King has recognized as the one he gave to Helena and placed on his own finger.

Parolles enters, and Bertram immediately confesses that the ring was Diana's. Under repeated questioning by the King, Parolles admits that he served as go-between for Bertram and Diana. Utterly baffled and confused by Diana's testimony about the ring, the King orders her to prison. At this point Diana sends her mother for Helena, and while she is gone Diana gives the King an enigmatic explanation of all that has happened.

To the amazement of all, Helena appears with the Widow. Pointing to Bertram's ring and declaring that she is with child by him, Helena asks Bertam if he will fulfill his promise to be her husband now that she has met his seemingly impossible conditions. Bertram promises to love Helena "ever, ever dearly," and in the general rejoicing Lafew accepts Parolles as his clown, and the King gives Diana a dower with which she may wed any man she chooses.

MEASURE FOR MEASURE [1603–1605]

CHARACTERS

VINCENTIO [*Friar Lodowick*], Duke of Vienna.

ANGELO, the Deputy.

ESCALUS, an ancient Lord.

CLAUDIO, a young gentleman.

LUCIO, a fantastic.

Two other like gentlemen.

PROVOST.

THOMAS,
PETER, } two friars.

A JUSTICE.

VARRIUS.[1]

ELBOW, a simple constable.

FROTH, a foolish gentleman.

POMPEY, a clown, servant to *Mistress Overdone*.

ABHORSON, an executioner.

BARNARDINE, a dissolute prisoner.

ISABELLA, sister to *Claudio*.

MARIANA, betrothed to *Angelo*.

JULIET, beloved of *Claudio*.

FRANCISCA, a nun.

MISTRESS OVERDONE, a bawd.

Lords, Officers, Citizens, Boy, and Attendants.

Scene: *Vienna*

I,i. The Duke's Palace

Vincentio tells his old adviser, Escalus, of his plan to leave the city and to appoint Angelo to rule as Deputy during his absence. When Angelo enters, the Duke praises his talents and virtues and assigns him absolute powers over Vienna. Modestly disclaiming any qualifications for the appointment, Angelo hesitates to accept the office, but the Duke insists and hastens away. Angelo and Escalus prepare to discuss Escalus's role as sub-deputy in the new administration.

---

[1] Varrius speaks no lines anywhere in the play.

I,ii. A Street

While Lucio and two other gentlemen are joking with one another, Mistress Overdone joins them and tells them that Claudio has been arrested for getting Juliet with child. Lucio and his companions scurry off to confirm her report, and Pompey appears. He confirms the rumor of Claudio's arrest and tells Mistress Overdone of the proclamation to remove all brothels from the environs of Vienna. When the bawd wonders what will become of her business, Pompey says that he will continue to be her pander. The two depart as the Provost, Claudio, Juliet, and officers approach, with Lucio and the two gentlemen following.[1]

Claudio protests against his public exposure as a prisoner, but the Provost declares that he is acting on specific orders from Angelo. Lucio asks Claudio the cause of his arrest. Claudio explains that he and Juliet delayed their intended marriage; in the meantime she has become pregnant, and Claudio is now charged with lechery under a long-neglected statute that Angelo, as Deputy, has suddenly resolved to enforce. Claudio requests Lucio to communicate his plight to Isabella, who is beginning her novitiate in a nunnery on this very day. Claudio hopes that she may plead to Angelo in his behalf.

I,iii. A Monastery

Vincentio requests sanctuary in the monastery. He explains to Friar Thomas that he wishes to disguise himself as a member of the order so that, incognito, he may observe Angelo's rigorous attempts to reform the lives of the Viennese, who have grown increasingly dissolute under his own lax enforcement of law.

I,iv. A Nunnery

Lucio interrupts Francisa's description to Isabella of convent life. Explaining that as a sworn nun she cannot speak with men except in the presence of the prioress, Francisca leaves Isabella to talk with the visitor. First doubting Lucio's account of Claudio's involvement with Juliet, Isabella finally suggests that her brother marry his sweetheart. Lucio then explains that the zealous Angelo, "whose blood/Is very snow-broth," has determined to make an example of Claudio and has signed orders for his execution. Now distraught, Isabella agrees to entreat Angelo for mercy.

---

[1] Some editors introduce a new scene at this point, thus providing for five scenes in Act I. The majority, however, accept a four-scene division of the act.

II,i. A Hall in Angelo's House

Escalus is pleading with Angelo to show clemency to Claudio, but Angelo insists that justice requires the young man's execution. The Deputy adds that when he commits a similar offense he will expect identical punishment. Angelo then orders the Provost to prepare Claudio for death at nine o'clock the following morning.

Elbow and his officers now haul Pompey and Froth before Angelo, Escalus, and the Justice. Elbow proceeds to charge Pompey with having enticed Mistress Elbow into Mistress Overdone's house for immoral purposes. Pompey denies the accusation and argues that Mistress Elbow entered the premises voluntarily to procure stewed prunes. Froth corroborates Pompey's story, but the testimony becomes so rambling and confused that Angelo leaves Escalus to complete the hearing. After listening to more evidence, Escalus warns Froth and releases him. Further interrogation of Pompey elicits his admission that he is a pimp, but he confidently predicts that no law can remove prostitution from Vienna. Thanking Pompey for his frank prophecy, Escalus says that he will have Pompey whipped if he is arrested again for any offense. Pompey thanks Escalus for his good counsel and leaves but indicates in an aside that he will continue his profession.

Escalus instructs Elbow to submit the names of six or seven members of his parish who might qualify as constables. Escalus and the Justice then deplore the impending death of Claudio.

II,ii. Another Room in Angelo's House

Feeling pity for Claudio and the "groaning Juliet," the Provost beseeches Angelo to revoke Claudio's death sentence, but the Deputy sternly orders the Provost to begone and do his office. The Provost lingers, however, as a servant introduces Lucio and Isabella.

Isabella pleads for leniency to Claudio, but Angelo remains cold, stern, and adamant to all her entreaties, arguing that the law, not he, condemns her brother. When Isabella inquires what other offenders have incurred the death penalty for the same crime, Angelo maintains that previous laxity in enforcing the law does not warrant or condone new violations. Reinforced by Lucio's whispered encouragements, Isabella pleads so eloquently that Angelo at last tells her to see him again the following day.

Angelo soliloquizes in an effort to evaluate the emotions Isabella has wakened in him. Admitting the propriety of Isabella's conduct, he senses a lustful desire for her. The possibility that he has instructed her to return merely in order to "feast upon her eyes" and the thought that he might mitigate Claudio's punishment disturb him.

II,iii. A Prison

Disguised as a friar, Vincentio tells the Provost that he has come to minister to the prisoners. Juliet walks in, and the Provost informs the Duke that the father of her unborn child is under sentence of death. Pretending to receive Juliet's confession and repentance, the Duke leaves her and goes to talk with Claudio.

II,iv. Angelo's House

Angelo has found efforts to pray fruitless because his evil plan to seduce Isabella dominates his thoughts. A servant announces her arrival. Angelo cuts Isabella's pleading short by asking her whether she would prefer to abandon Claudio to execution or save him by yielding her chastity. When she finally perceives the Deputy's intent, Isabella at once declares that she would forfeit her own life or that of Claudio to preserve her honor. Angelo reminds her that she previously argued that Claudio's affair with Juliet was more "A merriment than a vice." In plain words Angelo says that he loves her and that he will pardon Claudio if she will give her body to him. She threatens to expose him publicly, but he warns her that no one will believe her word against his. Saying that he will add torture to Claudio's punishment if she does not accede to his proposal, Angelo departs. Torn by her dilemma, Isabella resolves to seek Claudio's fraternal approval of her decision and "fit his mind to death for his soul's rest."

III,i. The Prison

Vincentio, in the guise of a friar, is preparing Claudio for his execution while the Provost stands guard. Calmed by the friar's philosophizing on life and death, Claudio accepts his fate as Isabella enters. Pulling the Provost aside, Vincentio conceals himself so that he may overhear the conversation between brother and sister.

In response to Claudio's questioning, Isabella tells him that the only alternative to his execution is one that will fetter him till death and divest him of all honor. Growing somewhat impatient at Isabella's generalizations, Claudio declares that if he must die he "will encounter darkness as a bride/And hug it" in his arms. Satisfied that Claudio is steadfast in honor and courage, Isabella tells him of Angelo's lecherous proposal.

Claudio's first reaction is to forbid his sister to yield herself to the wicked Deputy. Quickly, however, Claudio designates lechery as the least of the Seven Deadly Sins, and in highly vivid and imaginative words he describes the horrors and unknown perils of death. Unnerved by his own speech, he begs Isabella to consent to Angelo's invitation and thus save his life. Horrified and disgusted at Claudio's plea that she purchase his life with her virtue, Isabella denounces her brother as a "faithless coward" and "dishonest wretch" and says, " 'Tis best that thou diest quickly."

Stepping from his hiding place, Vincentio asks Isabella to wait for him. The Duke then tells Claudio that he has overheard the conversation and assures the young man that in his office of priestly confessor to Angelo he knows that the Deputy does not seriously plan to violate Isabella's chastity but is rather testing her to study human nature. Convinced that nothing can save him, Claudio seeks Isabella's pardon and leaves.

Dismissing the Provost, Vincentio asks Isabella what answer she plans to make to Angelo. Staunch in her resolution to preserve her honor, Isabella tells the supposed friar that she wishes she might inform the absent Duke of Angelo's villainy. Vincentio advises her that Angelo would deny her accusation and repeats his opinion that the Deputy is merely making trial of her. He then relates how Angelo broke his betrothal with Mariana because she lost her marriage portion when her brother Frederick drowned at sea. If Isabella grants Angelo's request for an assignation, the Duke suggests, she can introduce Mariana in her place. The Duke will make the arrangements with Mariana, and in this way Mariana may compel Angelo to marry her and Isabella can save the life of Claudio. Isabella willingly agrees to the plan, and they depart to make their preparations.

III,ii. The Street in Front of the Prison

Still is his borrowed vestment, the Duke encounters Elbow and his officers, who have arrested Pompey for pandering and carrying a picklock. The Duke upbraids Pompey for his occupation and tells Elbow to convey him to prison where correction and instruction may chasten him. Elbow says that Pompey must appear before Angelo, who has given the offender previous warning. When Lucio approaches, Pompey greets him as a friend and asks him to stand his bail, but Lucio approves Pompey's arrest and refuses help. Elbow and the officers remove Pompey to prison.

Lucio then interrogates the Friar (Vincentio) on the whereabouts of the Duke. When the cleric replies that he does not know, Lucio condemns Angelo's severity in applying the law and says that the Deputy is a male puppet rather than a real man. Lucio also tells the Friar that the former Duke at times engaged in immoral practices and "would be drunk too." The Friar accuses Lucio of misrepresenting his ruler, but Lucio insists that he really loves the Duke and that he will maintain his statements before the Duke's own person on his return. Again criticizing Angelo for his harshness and further slandering the Duke, Lucio leaves.

While the Duke sadly comments on the viciousness of calumny, Escalus, the Provost, and their officers appear with Mistress Overdone. Charged with operating a brothel, Mistress Overdone tells Escalus that Lucio has testified against her in order to avoid marrying his mistress and supporting his illegitimate child. Escalus orders the officers to remove Mistress Overdone and directs the Provost to furnish Claudio with spiritual advisers in preparation for his execution. The Provost replies that the Friar (the disguised Duke) has already talked with Claudio.

Vincentio introduces himself to Escalus as a religious brother who has recently arrived on special business from the Pope. He asks Escalus to characterize the absent Duke, but Escalus tersely describes him as "a gentleman of all temperance" and inquires about the welfare of Claudio, for whom he is presently much more concerned. Explaining that he has pleaded in vain with Angelo to reduce Claudio's sentence, Escalus leaves with the Provost to visit the doomed prisoner. Having observed that if Angelo's "own life answer the straitness of his proceeding, it shall become him well," the Duke then soliloquizes on Angelo's hypocrisy and resolves to expose the unworthiness of the Deputy.[1]

IV,i. The Moated Grange at Saint Luke's

Mariana listens to the Boy's melancholy love song and sends him away when the Duke approaches in his friar's robes. While Vincentio and Mariana exchange greetings, Isabella joins them. The Duke asks Mariana to leave while he learns Isabella's plans for

---

[1] Many editors regard this soliloquy (the last twenty-two lines of III,ii) as non-Shakespearian; others defend the speech as authentic.

keeping her assignation with Angelo that evening. The Duke recalls
Mariana, and she retires with Isabella, who informs her of the scheme
to deceive Angelo. In a moment the girls return, and the Duke (as
Friar) tells Mariana that he not only consents to her part in the plot
but entreats her to undertake it and says that she will be innocent
of any sin.

IV,ii. The Prison

Pompey agrees with the Provost to serve as Abhorson's assistant
in the beheading of Claudio and Barnardine the following morning.
The Provost summons Abhorson, who takes Pompey out for instructions. Expressing pity for Claudio but none for Barnardine, the con-
demned murderer, the Provost calls for the prisoners at midnight.
Claudio appears and tells the Provost that Barnardine is sleeping as
soundly as a weary traveler. Claudio departs, and the disguised Duke
enters to inquire if Isabella and her companions have arrived. While
the Duke chats with the Provost and indicates surprise that a coun-
termand for Claudio's execution has not come, a messenger appears
from Angelo with a document which the Duke assumes to be Claudio's
pardon. Instead, Angelo's order directs the Provost to move forward
Claudio's execution, to send him Claudio's head as proof of the deed,
and to behead Barnardine in the afternoon. Learning from the Provost
that Barnardine has confessed his crime and that he has maintained a
drunken disregard for his impending fate, the Duke (in his guise of
Friar) requests the Provost to substitute Barnardine's head for
Claudio's and stay Claudio's execution for a period of four days.
When the Provost protests that he cannot violate his oath of office
to the Duke, the supposed Friar produces "the hand and seal of
the Duke" as proof that he is acting with the sanction and approval
of the absent ruler.

IV,iii. The Prison

Pompey has found so many of Mistress Overdone's former customers in the prison that he feels himself completely at home. Abhorson enters and orders Pompey to produce Barnardine. When Pompey
calls him, the murderer replies from another room that he is sleepy
and wishes quiet. Barnardine then comes in and says that he is
not ready for death because he has been drinking all night. When
the Friar (Vincentio) appears and attempts to provide spiritual
consolation, Barnardine retires and says that the Friar may talk with

him in his cell because he will not leave it for the remainder of the day. Seeing that the murderer has no inclination to repent, Vincentio sends Pompey and Abhorson to carry out Barnardine's execution.

At this point, the Provost enters and inquires about Barnardine's state of mind. Learning from the disguised Duke that Barnardine is spiritually unready and unfit for death, the Provost tells the Duke that Ragozine, a notorious pirate, has that morning died of a fever and suggests that instead of beheading Barnardine they substitute Ragozine's head for Claudio's. Sending the Provost to carry out this new plan while he attempts to prepare Barnardine for a later execution, the Duke says that he will write Angelo of the ruler's imminent return to Vienna.

Dispatching the Provost with Ragozine's head to Angelo, the Duke decides to withhold from Isabella any word of the plan to save Claudio. Isabella comes in, and he tells her that Claudio's head is on its way to Angelo. He tries to allay her cries for revenge on Angelo with news of the Duke's early return. He also requests her to fetch Friar Peter to Mariana's house, where further arrangements will be made for Isabella to confront Angelo. Lucio appears and comforts the departing Isabella with the thought that the absent Duke would have spared her brother's life if he had been at home. Lucio once again contemns the Duke's character and admits his own rascality.

IV,iv. Angelo's House

Bewildered by the conflicting letters they have received from the Duke, Angelo and Escalus proclaim a public audience on the occasion of his impending return to the city. Escalus departs, and Angelo confesses remorse and shame for the dishonoring of Isabella and the death of Claudio, actions he supposes to have taken place.

IV,v. Fields Outside the Town

Vincentio, now in his own person as Duke, instructs Friar Peter and Varrius regarding preparations for his entry into Vienna.

IV,vi. Street near the City Gate

Isabella and Mariana are discussing how they will accuse Angelo of his misdeeds. Friar Peter offers to lead them to a place where they will be certain to get the Duke's attention.

V,i. The City Gate

Angelo and Escalus extend a public welcome to the Duke, who commends both of them for their competent governing of the city in his absence. Peter conducts Isabella before the Duke, and she appeals for justice against the wrongs Angelo has committed. At first the Duke appears to accept Angelo's comment that Isabella is out of her wits, but he decides to hear her story. While the Duke reprimands Lucio for his frequent efforts to corroborate Isabella's account, she reviews all that has happened. Upon conclusion of her recital, the Duke pretends to disbelieve all that she has said and orders an officer to take her to prison. He inquires if anyone knows of her purpose in denouncing Angelo, and Isabella wishes that Friar Lodowick (the name the Duke assumed in his disguise) were present.

When Vincentio asks if anyone knows Friar Lodowick, Lucio replies that he knows the Friar but dislikes him because he slandered the Duke. Friar Peter now steps forward to support the existence and character of the ill and missing Friar Lodowick, who has delegated Friar Peter to testify in the case for him. As guards lead Isabella away, Mariana enters veiled.

To the Duke's command that she show her face, Mariana says that she will not do so until her husband bids her to, but adds that she is neither virgin, married woman, nor widow. Lucio comments that she may be a prostitute, and the Duke silences him. Mariana testifies that Angelo was in her arms at the time Isabella accuses the Deputy of violating her. Unveiling herself, Mariana tells the puzzled Angelo that his assignation took place with her rather than with Isabella. Angelo admits his former betrothal to Mariana but insists that he has not seen her, spoken with her, or heard from her in five years. To this Mariana maintains that he has recently discharged the physical obligations of a husband with her. Angelo steadfastly proclaims his innocence, and the Duke tells him that he may punish both Mariana and Friar Peter for their malicious charges. After ordering the Provost to find and produce the missing Friar Lodowick, the Duke instructs Angelo and Escalus to continue their investigation of the slanderers and departs. Escalus sends for Isabella, who quickly appears with the Provost, officers, and the Duke (in his garb as Friar Lodowick).

When Escalus accuses Isabella and Friar Lodowick of slander against Angelo, the Friar retorts that the trial should properly take place before the Duke himself. As Friar Lodowick continues to impugn Angelo and the city of Vienna, Escalus orders him to prison. Lucio instantly seizes the opportunity to accuse Friar Lodowick of vilifying the Duke, thus adding to the abuse directed against the Friar.

Lucio plucks off Friar Lodowick's hood and exposes the Duke. Ordering the Provost to free Isabella, Mariana, and Friar Peter, and to seize Lucio, the Duke pardons Escalus and deposes Angelo from his role of judge. In reply to the Duke's outraged questions, Angelo confesses his guilt and asks for an immediate death sentence. After commanding the Provost to oversee Friar Peter's marriage of Angelo and Mariana, the Duke seeks Isabella's pardon for permitting Claudio's execution.

When the Provost and Friar Peter bring back the newly married Angelo and Mariana, the Duke declares that the law requires "Measure still for Measure" and orders the immediate decapitation of Angelo. Mariana's and Isabella's appeals for mercy fall on deaf ears as the Duke remains inflexible in this effecting of justice.

Remembering that Claudio was beheaded at an unusual hour, the Duke cashiers the Provost for violating his office, but the Provost asks permission for Barnardine to testify in his behalf. On the Duke's order, the Provost fetches Barnardine, Juliet, and a muffled prisoner who, he says, resembles Claudio. After pardoning Barnardine and committing him to Friar Peter for rehabilitation, the Duke also pardons the unmuffled Claudio for the sake of the lovely Isabella, to whom he proposes marriage. Unable to excuse the slanderous Lucio, Vincentio first orders that he be whipped and hanged but then relents and sentences him to wed the harlot who has borne his illegitimate child. Swiftly the Duke commands Claudio to marry Juliet, fully pardons Angelo with the exhortation to love Mariana and treat her well, thanks Escalus for his goodness, and promotes the Provost for faithful service.

PERICLES, PRINCE OF TYRE[1] [1608–1609]

CHARACTERS

GOWER, as Chorus.

ANTIOCHUS, King of Antioch.

PERICLES, Prince of Tyre.

HELICANUS,
ESCANES, } two lords of Tyre.

SIMONIDES, King of Pentapolis.

CLEON, Governor of Tharsus.

LYSIMACHUS, Governor of Mytilene.

CERIMON, a lord of Ephesus.

THALIARD, a lord of Antioch.

PHILEMON, servant to *Cerimon*.

LEONINE, servant to *Dionyza*.

Marshal.

A Pander.

BOULT, his servant.

The Daughter of *Antiochus*.

DIONYZA, wife to *Cleon*.

THAISA, daughter to *Simonides*.

MARINA, daughter to *Pericles* and *Thaisa*.

LYCHORIDA, nurse to *Marina*.

A Bawd.

DIANA.

Lords, Ladies, Knights, Gentlemen, Sailors, Fishermen [*Pilch, Patchbreech*], Messengers.

Scene: *Antioch; Tyre; Tharsus; Pentapolis; a Ship at Sea; Ephesus; Mytilene*

I, Prologue. Antioch. In Front of the Palace of Antiochus

Gower, a fourteenth-century English poet, summarizes the story of Antiochus the Great, who, in order to preserve an incestuous relationship with his own daughter, confronted her suitors with a riddle.

---

[1] Although *Pericles* does not appear in the First Folio (1623) or the Second Folio (1632), most authorities admit it to the canon of Shakespeare's works. The majority of critics and editors agree, however, that an unknown author wrote most of Acts I and II and that Shakespeare was responsible for substantially all of Acts III–V.

126

Anyone who could solve the riddle would win the daughter's hand, but everyone who failed to answer it forfeited his life.

I,i. Antioch. The Palace of Antiochus

Pericles declares that he is ready to risk his life to win the hand of Antiochus's daughter. Music plays, and the King commands his Daughter to enter. While Pericles praises the Daughter's beauty, Antiochus points to the heads of suitors who have failed and warns him to abandon the test. Confidently Pericles persists. The Daughter wishes him happiness, and Antiochus hands him the riddle to read. Quickly discerning that the riddle describes the illicit love between Antiochus and his Daughter, Pericles replies in equivocal phrases which indicate to Antiochus that he has found the solution. Privately amazed and wishing that he could get rid of Pericles, Antiochus says that the young man has misinterpreted the enigma but may have an extension of forty days in which to find the true answer.

In a soliloquy, Pericles enlarges on the terms of the riddle and, now fully aware of the ruthless character of the King, determines to leave Antioch at once.

No sooner has Pericles departed than Antiochus appears, summons Thaliard, and bribes him to poison Pericles before he can publish the King's infamy. A messenger announces that Pericles has fled, and Antiochus commands Thaliard to pursue the Prince and murder him.

I,ii. Tyre. The Palace

Dismissing his attendants, Pericles reflects on the probability that Antiochus will relentlessly harass him, even to the point of invading Tyre and punishing many innocent people. The lords return to pay their duty to the Prince; he sends them all out except Helicanus, with whom he reviews the dangerous discovery he made in Antioch and the likelihood that Antiochus will undertake reprisals. Helicanus agrees that Pericles has ample reason to fear the tyrant and approves the Prince's wish to forestall war between Antioch and Tyre. On the advice of his faithful lord, whom he delegates as ruler in his absence, Pericles determines to leave Tyre and go to Tharsus.

I,iii. Tyre. The Palace

Thaliard, the hired killer, arrives in Tyre on his dangerous mission. He overhears the conversation of Helicanus, Escanes, and other lords, and learns that Pericles has fled by sea. Thaliard identifies himself as an envoy from Antiochus to Pericles but says, "Now message must return from whence it came."

I,iv. Tharsus. The House of the Governor

Cleon and Dionyza, in the presence of their attendants, are lamenting the severe famine that has seized the city of Tharsus. A lord enters with news of a fleet's arrival. Discouraged, Cleon fears a hostile invasion, but the lord says that the ships are flying white flags of truce. "Welcome is peace, if he on peace consist;/If wars, we are unable to resist," Cleon declares as he instructs the lord to bring the visitor before him. Pericles appears with his followers and reveals that his vessels are filled with grain for the starving city. All bow in gratitude; however, Pericles says that he does not look for reverence but seeks harborage for himself, his ships, and his men. Cleon extends the newcomers a hearty welcome.

II, Prologue

Briefly summarizing the events of Act I, Gower introduces a *Dumb Show* that pantomimes Pericles receiving a letter from Helicanus. Gower explains that the letter reports Thaliard's attempt to murder Pericles in Tyre and advises him to flee Tharsus. Again Pericles puts out to sea but encounters a storm from which he is the sole survivor.

II,i. Pentapolis. An Open Place by the Seaside

Wet and exhausted, Pericles picks himself up from the rocks and craves only to die in peace. Three fishermen (two of whom are named Pilch and Patchbreech) appear with their nets. They have witnessed the drowning of Pericles's companions in the storm, and they regret that they were unable to help them. Learning from their homespun philosophizing and comments that he is in the land of King Simonides, Pericles appeals to the fishermen for clothing, food, and shelter. While two of the fishermen are hauling in their net, the other one tells Pericles that they are within half a day's journey of Pentapolis, where an assembly of suitors will joust the next day in celebration of the princess's birthday.

At this moment the fishermen pull in their net and discover that they have recovered Pericles's own suit of armor from the sea. Regarding this stroke of fortune as a good omen, Pericles resolves to enter the tournament on the following day. The fishermen give him the armor and promise to provide him with other garments and conduct him to Pentapolis.

II,ii. Pentapolis. A Public Street and a Pavilion near the Lists

Simonides, Thaisa, and attendants appear, and the King orders a lord to present the contestants in the tournament. Five knights parade in succession before Thaisa; their pages display their crests and mottoes to Thaisa, and she describes them in turn. A sixth knight (Pericles), in rusty armor and unaccompanied, offers his emblem directly to Thaisa:

> A withered branch that's only green at top;
> The motto, 'In hac spe vivo' [In this hope I live].

Various lords make disparaging remarks about the last knight's mean array, but Simonides cautions against judging the inner man by outward appearance. All go to the lists, from which come shouts of "The mean knight!"

II,iii. Pentapolis. A Hall of State. A Banquet Prepared

In the presence of his court, Simonides welcomes to the feast the knights who have engaged in the tilting. Thaisa gives Pericles the victory wreath. Curious as to the identity of Pericles and impressed with his dignified and melancholy manner, Simonides and Thaisa lose their appetite for food. Toasting Pericles, Simonides orders Thaisa, who feigns a coy reluctance, to address the knight and inquire his home, name, and parentage. Modestly, Pericles identifies himself as a gentleman of Tyre who has suffered shipwreck. Pitying his guest's misfortune, Simonides calls for a dance. Commending Pericles on his skill as a dancer, the King instructs his attendants to conduct the knights to their "several lodgings" and aranges for Pericles to stay in quarters next his own. Advising that "it is too late to talk of love," Simonides says that the knights can turn to this purpose on the morrow and bids them all good night.

II,iv. Tyre. The House of Helicanus, the Governor

Helicanus informs Escanes that an outraged heaven has destroyed Antiochus and his Daughter, both of whom have died for their gross sins. Two or three lords appear. Impatient under the absence of Pericles, they urge Helicanus to produce Pericles or assume the throne himself. Faithful to his prince, the regent is unwilling to accept the office of sovereign and persuades the lords to set forth on a search for the missing Pericles.

II,v. Pentapolis. The Palace of Simonides

Simonides, reading a letter, tells the knights present that Thaisa has vowed to retain her virginity for twelve months and that they cannot hope to see her. They leave, and the King discloses Thaisa's written determination to marry Pericles, a choice in which he concurs.

Dissembling, Simonides first tells Pericles that he must tutor Thaisa; then he accuses the Prince of bewitching the Princess and of being a villainous traitor. Pericles vehemently denies the accusation as Thaisa appears and joyously accepts his love. After teasing the young couple briefly, Simonides gives his blessing to their immediate marriage.

III, Prologue

Gower reveals that Thaisa and Pericles are expecting the birth of a child. The *Dumb Show* pantomimes the departure of the couple from Pentapolis. Gower explains that upon receiving news of the demise of Antiochus and his Daughter and of the attempt of certain lords to enthrone Helicanus in Tyre if the rightful ruler does not return within a year, Pericles sails for home. The pregnant Thaisa and Lychorida, a nurse, accompany him. Once again Pericles runs into a violent storm at sea.

III,i. Shipboard

Thaisa is in labor, and Pericles calls for Lychorida. The Nurse appears with an infant, the daughter of Pericles, and says that Thaisa has died in childbirth. Torn between joy at the birth of his child and grief at the death of his wife, Pericles listens while two sailors state their belief that the storm will not abate until they have cast Thaisa's corpse into the sea. Pericles commits the infant to Lychorida's care and prepares to place Thaisa's body along with jewels and money in a watertight chest that the sailors have ready for the purpose. Afraid that his little daughter cannot survive the long voyage to Tyre, Pericles orders the sailors to make for Tharsus, where he will entrust her to Cleon's care.

III,ii. Ephesus. The House of Cerimon

Cerimon and his servant, Philemon, busy themselves in caring for some poor shipwrecked men. After doing what he can for them,

Cerimon dismisses them and sends Philemon on an errand to the apothecary. Two gentlemen, disturbed by the violence of the recent storm, enter and express their surprise at finding Cerimon up and about so early. He explains that he is engrossed in his research and practice of medicine. The gentlemen praise Cerimon's skill in effecting miraculous cures and laud his generosity in effort and money to his fellow citizens.

At this point two or three servants carry in a chest which one of the gentlemen says resembles a coffin. When the servants report that the sea tossed the chest ashore, Cerimon commands them to open it. Inside they discover the body of Thaisa with a scroll from Pericles requesting a decent burial for the corpse by whoever happens to find the chest and offering the jewels and treasure for a fee. Seeing the freshness of the corpse, Cerimon sends for prescriptions, cloths, and fire. To the sound of music, he successfully restores Thaisa to consciousness. Knowing that a relapse would prove fatal, Cerimon removes Thaisa to an adjoining room.

III,iii. Tharsus. The House of Cleon

Compelled to hasten on to Tyre, Pericles leaves Marina under the care and training of Cleon and Dionyza, who promise to rear her faithfully. Pericles bids his friends farewell and tells Lychorida to look to her little mistress.

III,iv. Ephesus. The House of Cerimon

Thaisa, who has no recollection of delivering a child at sea and believes that she will never see Pericles again, tells Cerimon that she will embrace a life of celibacy in the nearby temple of Diana.

IV, Prologue

Gower summarizes intervening action. Pericles has arrived in Tyre. Thaisa is a votaress of Diana in Ephesus. Lychorida is dead. Marina has matured in all feminine graces, but Dionyza, envious because she overshadows Philoten (daughter of Cleon and Dionyza) in every respect, plots Marina's murder.

IV,i. Tharsus. A Place near the Seashore

Leonine assures Dionyza that he will follow her instructions and kill the fourteen-year-old Marina, who is approaching them with a basket of flowers. Chiding Marina for her melancholy manner, Dionyza orders her to walk along the strand with Leonine. Dionyza

departs, and Marina chatters with Leonine about the stories Lychorida told of the storm in which she was born. Abruptly, Leonine
orders Marina to say her prayers and prepare for death. She appeals
to his better nature, but he replies that he has sworn to commit the
deed. As he seizes her, Pirates suddenly appear, frighten Leonine,
and carry Marina off to their ship. Returning, Leonine identifies
them as marauders in the service of the pirate Valdes. Entertaining
no hope for Marina's return, Leonine first resolves to report her
death; then he decides to wait to see if the Pirates ravish her and
put her ashore. If they do, he must kill her then.

IV,ii. Mytilene. A Brothel

Finding their house reduced to three harlots and knowing that the
town is full of would-be clients, the Pander and the Bawd order
Boult to search the market for replacements. While Boult is away,
the Pander argues with the Bawd that they should take their profits
and retire from their hazardous business.

Boult returns with the Pirates and Marina, for whom the rogues
are demanding a thousand pieces. Leaving with the Pirates to get
the money, the Pander tells his wife (the Bawd) to instruct Marina
in her new occupation. The Bawd orders Boult to advertise Marina's
specifications "with warrant of her virginity," an asset that should
command a higher fee. Boult leaves, and Marina bewails her fate to
the unsympathetic Bawd.

To Marina's increasing horror, Boult reappears and describes the
eagerness with which numerous customers are anticipating enjoying
her favors. The Bawd advises Marina on how to entice more profit
from her clients, but the innocent girl fails to understand. Promising
Boult that he may give Marina practical training in her new profession, the Bawd orders him to return to the town and solicit more
business. Marina vows to preserve her virginity at any cost and
invokes Diana's aid, but the Bawd says, "What have we to do with
Diana?" and commands the girl to follow her.

IV,iii. Tharsus. The House of Cleon

Cleon is rebuking Dionyza for the supposed poisoning of Marina.
Dionyza maintains that, since Leonine is gone, no one will ever know
the truth of Marina's death; furthermore, they have prepared an
expensive monument praising Marina in "glitt'ring golden characters."

IV,iv. In Front of the Monument of Marina at Tharsus

Gower enters and explains that Pericles and Helicanus have left Tyre under the governorship of Escanes while they journey to see Marina. A *Dumb Show* pantomimes Pericles weeping at the tomb of Marina and then parting from Cleon and Dionyza "in a mighty passion." Gower goes on to explain that Pericles, swearing "Never to wash his face nor cut his hairs," has donned sackcloth and put to sea. He encounters another storm, which he succeeds in riding out. Gower then reads Dionyza's hypocritical epitaph for Marina and notes that Pericles believes Marina to be dead.

IV,v. Mytilene. A Street in Front of the Brothel

Two gentlemen emerge from the brothel and profess themselves reformed by Marina's preaching.

IV,vi. Mytilene. A Room in the Brothel

Confounded by Marina's gradual reformation of their clients, the Pander, the Bawd, and Boult decide that they must either rape Marina or get rid of her. At this point Lysimachus, Governor of Mytilene, appears in disguise, although the keepers of the house recognize him.

Boasting of his physical health, Lysimachus inquires if the procurers can supply him with a virgin who will not infect him. Boult ushers in Marina, and the Bawd informs the girl of the position and wealth of her customer. Alone with Lysimachus, Marina so impresses him with her speech and virtue that he spares her chastity, rewards her handsomely, and urges her to persevere in preserving her honor.

Boult asks a tip of the departing Lysimachus, but the Governor curses the pimp and his evil house. Crying that he will ravish the unhappy girl, Boult explains to the Bawd that Marina has deterred Lysimachus in his lustful purposes. The Bawd tells Boult to use Marina at his pleasure and to overcome her prudishness.

While Boult is preparing to assault her, Marina bribes him to intercede with the proprietors of the house for her and to persuade them to hire her out in decent employment "amongst honest women." Boult agrees to do what he can for her.

V, Prologue

Gower tells how Marina gains her release from the brothel and toils at humble but respectable chores, the Bawd taking her wages.

Meanwhile, winds have driven Pericles to Mytilene, where Lysimachus prepares to go aboard the Tyrian ship.

V,i. The Ship of Pericles, off Mytilene

Helicanus directs some of his gentlemen to welcome Lysimachus
aboard. Helicanus explains that Pericles is in the ship but that he
has been prostrate with grief and has not spoken to anyone for the
past three months. With the consent of Helicanus, Lysimachus addresses Pericles, who is reclining on a couch. When this effort to
rouse Pericles fails, Lysimachus approves the suggestion of one of
his lords and sends for "a maid in Mytilene" who "with her sweet
harmony/And other chosen attractions" may induce Pericles to talk.
While they await the arrival of this maid, Lysimachus agrees to
reprovision Pericles's ship.

A lord ushers in Marina and another young lady. Praising Marina
as one whom he would delight to marry, Lysimachus appeals to her
to employ all her skill to elicit speech from Pericles. First with a
song, which has no effect, and then with gentle words, Marina coaxes
Pericles into conversing with her. Gradually Pericles sees in Marina
a resemblance to his long lost wife. Imagining that his daughter might
have grown up to resemble Marina, Pericles inquires about her family
and origin.

Pericles's amazement grows as Marina tells him her name, says
that she is of royal birth and that her mother died immediately after
giving birth at sea, and adds that she learned these facts from
her "good nurse Lychorida." Pericles presses her for more details, and
she rapidly describes her departure from Tharsus and arrival in
Mytilene. Weeping, Pericles calls Helicanus and Lysimachus and
owns Marina as his daughter. Overcome with excitement and joy,
Pericles imagines that he hears "The music of the spheres . . . Most
heavenly music," and falls into a peaceful sleep. In a dream Diana
appears to him and commands him to hasten to her temple in
Ephesus, there to sacrifice and mourn his and Marina's trials and
hardships.

Waking, Pericles summons Helicanus, who enters with Lysimachus
and Marina. Pericles countermands his previous order to sail for
Tharsus to take revenge on Cleon and Dionyza and says that he will
proceed to Ephesus. Lysimachus offers generous supplies and intimates that he will seek the hand of Marina in marriage.

V,ii. Ephesus. In Front of the Temple of Diana

Gower summarizes the pageantry in Mytilene, the sacrificial services in Ephesus, and the betrothal of Marina and Lysimachus.

V,iii. Ephesus. The Temple of Diana

Pericles and other worshipers stand at the altar of Diana while Pericles identifies himself and recounts the remarkable sequence of events that have happened to him and his daughter. When he ends his recital, Thaisa, who as High Priestess has been standing near the altar with a number of vestals attending her, faints.

Pericles cries for help for the nun, but Cerimon declares that she is really Thaisa and tells how he removed her from the chest and restored her to life and health. Thaisa regains consciousness, and with excitement and joy she confirms their mutual recognition with a ring.

Amid general rejoicing, Pericles introduces Helicanus to Thaisa and then secures Cerimon's promise to explain his knowledge and power of healing. Announcing the approaching marriage of Lysimachus and Marina in Pentapolis, Pericles directs that they will reign in Tyre and that he and Thaisa will ascend the throne of Simonides, who has died. All depart, Pericles to trim his beard, which no razor has touched for fourteen years.

Gower briefly lists the moral lessons illustrated in the experiences of the principal characters and adds the information that Pericles razes Tharsus and burns Cleon and Dionyza in their palace for their intended murder of Marina.

CYMBELINE [1609–1610]

CHARACTERS

CYMBELINE, King of Britain.

CLOTEN, son to the *Queen* by a former husband.

POSTHUMUS LEONATUS, a gentleman, husband to *Imogen*.

BELARIUS, a banished lord, disguised under the name of *Morgan*.

GUIDERIUS, ARVIRAGUS, } sons to *Cymbeline*, disguised under the names of *Polydore* and *Cadwal*, supposed sons to *Morgan*.

PHILARIO, friend to *Posthumus*, IACHIMO, friend to *Philario*, } Italians.

A French Gentleman, friend to *Philario*.

CAIUS LUCIUS, General of the Roman forces.

A Roman Captain.

Two British Captains.

PISANIO, servant to *Posthumus*.

CORNELIUS, a physician.

Two Lords of *Cymbeline's* court.

Two Gentlemen of the same.

Two Jailors.

QUEEN, wife to *Cymbeline*.

IMOGEN [FIDELE], daughter to *Cymbeline* by a former queen.

HELEN, a lady attending on *Imogen*.

Apparitions.

Lords, Ladies [*Dorothy*], Roman Senators, Tribunes, a Soothsayer [*Philarmonus*], a Dutch Gentleman, a Spanish Gentleman, Musicians, Officers, Captains, Soldiers, Messengers, Attendants.

Scene: *Britain; Italy*

I,i. Britain. The Garden of Cymbeline's Palace

Two gentlemen are discussing the marriage of Imogen to Posthumus, an accomplished and exemplary orphan who has been living under the protection of the King. Cymbeline, whose two sons were kidnaped from the royal nursery some twenty years before, wished Imogen to wed her stepbrother Cloten. Vexed by his daughter's action, the King has decreed Posthumus's banishment and Imogen's imprisonment. The gentlemen break off their gossip and leave as the Queen, Posthumus, and Imogen enter.[1]

Pretending to befriend the young couple, the Queen risks Cymbeline's displeasure by leaving them to chat together, but she secretly resolves to betray them to the King. Imogen, fearing that her father's rage will vent itself more grievously on Posthumus than upon her, bids for husband farewell. Pledging his loyalty to her, Posthumus tells Imogen to write him in Rome, where he will live with Philario. The Queen returns and urges the pair to make haste before the King discovers them; she then leaves to make certain that the King will find them.

Lingering, Imogen gives Posthumus a ring as a parting favor, and he places a bracelet on her arm. At this moment Cymbeline appears with his attending lords. Angrily, he banishes Posthumus on pain of death and upbraids Imogen for preferring Posthumus to Cloten. The Queen returns and pretends to intercede for the Princess, but Cymbeline departs outraged. Pisanio, Posthumus's servant, comes in with word that his master has assigned him to remain in Imogen's service. He also relates how Cloten attacked the departing Posthumus, who parried his sword thrusts until gentlemen separated them. Imogen insists that Pisiano go to see Posthumus embark.

I,ii. Britain. A Public Place

Cloten is blustering with two lords concerning his recent altercation with Posthumus. In a series of asides, the Second Lord exposes Cloten's comic stupidity and boastfulness.

I,iii. Britain. Cymbeline's Palace

Pisanio describes to Imogen how he stood and watched Posthumus sail out of sight. She asks how soon she can hope to hear from Posthumus and reviews the parting phrases she did not have

[1] Editors vary in their division of scenes here and elsewhere in *Cymbeline*. This synopsis follows the pattern accepted by the majority of critics.

time to utter before he left. A lady summons Imogen to the Queen, and the Princess dispatches Pisanio on private errands.

I,iv. Rome. Philario's House

Philario, Iachimo, a Frenchman, a Dutchman, and a Spaniard are talking about Posthumus and the reasons for his visit to Philario. When Posthumus enters, he and the Frenchman recall a bitter argument when Posthumus stoutly boasted that his English sweetheart was superior in beauty, chastity, and other virtues to any of the ladies of France. Iachimo thereupon objects that Posthumus cannot similarly rate her above the ladies of Italy. Although Philario attempts to check the discussion, the argument grows more heated until Iachimo wagers ten thousand ducats against Posthumus's diamond ring that he can seduce Imogen. Despite Philario's protests, Iachimo and Posthumus depart to employ a lawyer to draw up the articles of the bet, Posthumus observing that if Imogen yields she is not worth their debate and if she proves faithful he will challenge Iachimo for having an ill opinion of her.

I,v. Britain. Cymbeline's Palace

After the Queen sends her attendants to gather flowers, Cornelius produces a box of prescriptions that the Queen has commanded him to prepare. When he inquires her reason for wanting them, she replies that she will test them on creatures "not worth the hanging (but none human)." Upon the appearance of Pisanio, Cornelius reveals in an aside that he has been suspicious of the Queen's motives and has given her powerful soporifics only, not potions fatal to animal or man. After the doctor has gone, the Queen exhorts Pisanio to persuade Imogen that Posthumus will not return and that she may as well entertain Cloten's suit. At the same time the Queen gives Pisanio the box of prescriptions as a reward for his service; she implies that the drugs are powerful restoratives. In an aside, Pisanio states that he suspects the Queen's motives and will remain loyal to Posthumus.

I,vi. Britain. Cymbeline's Palace

While Imogen is reviewing her unhappy situation and lamenting that she was not kidnaped as her brothers were, Pisanio introduces Iachimo as a friend of Posthumus. Reading the letter that Iachimo delivers, Imogen welcomes him cordially. Expressing admiration for Imogen's beauty and intellect, Iachimo sends Pisanio on an errand

and proceeds to represent Posthumus as a dissolute reveler forgetful of his marriage vows and unworthy of his wife. Iachimo urges Imogen to admit him to her bed and thus take revenge on her wayward husband. Indignantly, Imogen calls for Pisanio, denounces Iachimo for his improper advances, and declares that she will inform the King of the Italian's assault against her virtue. Reacting quickly to her display of loyalty and integrity, Iachimo insists that he has been merely testing her character in order to return and reassure Posthumus, who has really been conducting himself in exemplary fashion.

Imogen accepts Iachimo's apologies, whereupon he asks if she will act as custodian of a trunk filled with "plate of rare device, and jewels" which he and several friends have purchased as a gift for the Emperor. He adds that he must depart on the morrow and will gladly bear any letter Imogen may wish to write to Posthumus. Imogen tells him to send the trunk to her bedchamber, where "it shall safe be kept."

II,i. Britain. In Front of Cymbeline's Palace

Cloten, quarrelsome and irritable, chats with the two lords about a recent gambling melee. Informed of Iachimo's arrival, Cloten departs with the First Lord to recoup his losses at the Italian's expense. In a short soliloquy, the Second Lord marvels that the crafty Queen could "yield the world this ass!" and sympathizes with Imogen, who is surrounded by a henpecked father, a scheming stepmother, and a hateful wooer in the person of Cloten. He hopes that she will withstand all perils and remain faithful to Posthumus.

II,ii. Britain. Imogen's Bedchamber in the Palace

It is near midnight, and Imogen, weary from three hours of reading, instructs Helen to leave the candle burning and to call her at four o'clock. Helen retires; Imogen quickly falls asleep; and Iachimo creeps from a trunk in the corner of the bedroom.

Iachimo briefly comments on the beauty of the sleeping Princess; then he methodically writes down a description of her bedroom and its furnishings. Imogen's sleep is so sound that Iachimo removes the bracelet from her arm without waking her. He also notices a distinctive mole on her left breast. Recognizing that he now has sufficient evidence to convince anyone that he has seduced Imogen, Iachimo returns to the trunk as the clock strikes three.

II,iii. The Palace. An Anteroom adjoining Imogen's Apartments

Cloten, who has again lost at gaming, enters with the two lords and arranges for the musicians to render "Hark, hark! the lark at heaven's gate sings" for Imogen's benefit. The musicians depart as Cymbeline and the Queen enter and encourage Cloten in his courtship of his reluctant stepsister. A messenger appears and announces the arrival of Caius Lucius, ambassador from Rome. All leave except Cloten, who knocks on Imogen's door and tries to bribe one of her attendants. Imogen herself enters, and the lady departs.

Cloten protests his love for Imogen, but she stoutly rebuffs him and compares him unfavorably with Posthumus. Weary of Cloten's nagging, she summons Pisanio, tells him that she is haunted by a fool, and asks him to undertake a search for her missing bracelet. Pisiano withdraws, and Cloten threatens revenge for the insulting remarks Imogen has addressed to him.

II,iv. Rome. Philario's House

Posthumus expresses to Philario his confidence in Imogen's honor. The friends then discuss the possible outcome of Caius Lucius's mission demanding tribute from Cymbeline. Philario believes that the King will capitulate, but Posthumus predicts that the British, now better disciplined than when Julius Caesar invaded England, will resist by war.

At this moment Iachimo arrives with the statement that he has won his wager with Posthumus. Angrily, Posthumus demands positive proof. Iachimo first describes in detail the appointments of Imogen's bedchamber, but Posthumus objects that his rival could have learned these through hearsay. Iachimo then shows Posthumus the bracelet, which he declares Imogen gave him as a love token. Persuaded that Iachimo is telling the truth, Posthumus hands Iachimo his ring and admits defeat. Philario, however, suggests that Imogen may have lost the bracelet or that one of her women may have stolen it from her. As Philario tries to calm the doubting and distraught Posthumus, Iachimo describes the mole on Imogen's breast [1] and vows that he kissed it. This convinces both Posthumus and Philario of Imogen's guilt, and Posthumus dashes out declaring that he will "tear her limbmeal . . . i'th' court, before/Her father." Fearing that Post-

[1] In II,ii, Iachimo says that the mole is *on* her left breast; in II,iv, he says that it is *under* her breast.

humus may inflict injury upon himself, Philario and Iachimo follow him.

II,v. Rome. Philario's House [1]

Beside himself with disillusionment and rage, Posthumus reflects that all people, including himself, are bastards, and that women are responsible for every vice in man. Cynically he resolves to "write against them./Detest them, curse them."

III,i. Britain. Cymbeline's Palace

Cymbeline and members of the court hear Caius Lucius's demand for Rome's annual levy of three thousand pounds. Encouraged by the Queen's and Cloten's defiance of the ambassador, Cymbeline rejects Augustus Caesar's ultimatum and tells Caius Lucius that the Britons will fight for their independence. Having received Lucius's declaration of war, Cymbeline and Cloten invite the Roman general to remain as a welcome private guest.

III,ii. Britain. Another Room in Cymbeline's Palace

Pisanio is reading Posthumus's letter charging Imogen with adultery and commanding him to murder her. Convinced that some "false Italian" has deceived Posthumus, Pisanio states, "I am ignorant in what I am commanded." Imogen joins him, and he gives her another letter from Posthumus. In it Posthumus describes himself as "loyal to his vow" and says that he has landed at Milford Haven in Wales. Eager to join her returning husband, Imogen directs Pisanio to prepare for their immediate departure from court to meet him.

III,iii. Wales. A Mountainous Country with a Cave

Belarius is trying to persuade Guiderius and Arviragus that the wild and rugged life they lead is superior to that of the city and court. Belarius recounts how Cymbeline banished him on a false charge of treason twenty years before. Sending the two boys to hunt venison, Berlarius soliloquizes on how he kidnaped the lads when they were three and two years old respectively. Cymbeline now regards the princes as dead, and they accept Belarius under the name of Morgan as their natural father. Every day they honor the grave of their nurse Euriphile, whom they took for their mother.

---

[1] Some editors regard the soliloquy that follows as a continuation of scene iv rather than as a new scene.

III,iv. Britain (Wales). Near Milford Haven

Imogen is chiding Pisanio because they have not reached Post-humus. In reply, Pisanio shows her Posthumus's letter charging her with adultery and commanding the servant to kill her. Excited and frustrated by the false accusation, Imogen urges Pisanio to carry out his master's orders and slay her. When the faithful servant repeats his faith in her and loyalty to her, Imogen demands to know why he has accompanied her on their apparently fruitless journey. Pisanio explains that he has been playing for time in order to devise a plan of action. He suggests that he return to court with news and evi-ence of her death. Meanwhile Imogen can disguise herself as a man and enter the service of Caius Lucius so that she can be near Posthu-mus. In anticipation of the scheme, Pisanio has brought along "doub-let, hat, hose." Imogen quickly agrees, and as they part Pisanio gives her the box of prescriptions with the assurance that a dram will prove a sovereign remedy for any sickness or distemper.

III,v. Britain. Cymbeline's Palace

Cymbeline and his court bid a cordial farewell to Lucius, who regrets that he must carry the declaration of war to his emperor. Cymbeline grants Lucius safe-conduct to Milford Haven. The King, the Queen, and Cloten set about preparations for the coming Roman attack. Noting Imogen's absence, Cymbeline sends an attendant to fetch her. In the confusion that follows they decide that Imogen has locked her apartment and fled. While Cloten alone remains, Pisanio appears and hands him a letter which apparently divulges Post-humus's arrival at Milford Haven. As Cloten reads the letter, Pisanio resolves to advise Posthumus of Imogen's death.

Cloten, determined to kill Posthumus and ravish Imogen, bribes the apparently cooperative Pisanio to bring him a suit of Posthumus's clothes. Still firm in believing Posthumus honorable and acting under a misconception, and also resolute in his determination to protect Imogen, Pisanio pretends to accept employment with Cloten.

III,vi. Wales. In Front of the Cave of Belarius

Imogen, lost, tired, hungry, and discouraged, discovers the cave and hesitatingly calls to anyone who may be inside. Receiving no answer, she draws her sword and enters.[1]

---

[1] A few editors follow the First Folio division and provide for a new scene at this point. The majority continue scene vi.

Belarius, addressing the two princes as Polydore and Cadwal, says that he and Arviragus will play cook and servant to Guiderius, who has proved the most successful hunter and by agreement is master of the feast. Looking in the cave for cold meat to stanch their immediate hunger, Belarius discovers Imogen, who now appears.

Declaring that she is innocent of any wrongdoing, Imogen offends her hosts by offering them gold. In reply to their questions she identifies herself as Fidele and says that she is on her way to Milford. Reassuring Imogen (whom they suppose to be a young man) that they are friends, the three welcome her to their food and shelter.

III,vii. Rome. A Public Place

Roman Senators and Tribunes discuss the Emperor's commission to send reinforcements to Lucius to prosecute the war against Cymbeline.

IV,i. Wales. Near the Cave of Belarius

Cloten, arrayed in Posthumus's clothes and comparing himself favorably with their true owner, has tied his horse and is continuing to search for Posthumus and Imogen.

IV,ii. Wales. In Front of the Cave of Belarius

Belarius and the two boys, preparing for the morning hunt, urge the ailing Fidele to stay in the cave. Guiderius offers to remain with their guest, but Fidele insists that he can manage well enough in their absence. Before they leave him, he privately takes one of the drugs from Pisanio's box and returns to the cave.

At this moment, Cloten appears mumbling about the runagates (Posthumus and Imogen), whom he has been unable to locate. Overhearing Cloten and recognizing him as the Queen's son, Belarius assumes that the Prince is looking for him and the two kidnaped sons of the King. Sending Belarius and his brother to reconnoiter, Guiderius challenges Cloten and goads him into personal combat. They disappear fighting, as Belarius, and Arviragus return after assuring themselves that Cloten is unaccompanied.

Guiderius comes back with Cloten's head and explains that he killed his opponent in self-defense. Greatly alarmed by what has happened and fearing reprisals, Belarius calls off the hunt after Guiderius has thrown Cloten's head into the creek. While Belarius ponders these events, he hears strains of music from an "ingenious instrument" that has not produced a sound since the death of Euriphile. Belarius and Guiderius speculate as to why Arviragus has chosen this moment to play the instrument. Their puzzlement changes to grief when Arviragus appears carrying the apparently dead Fidele in his arms. Sadly, the brothers cover Fidele's body with flowers beside the grave of Euriphile and sing a dirge. Belarius brings in the headless corpse of Cloten and deposits it beside Fidele. After strewing flowers on the second body, Belarius and the princes depart.

Regaining consciousness, Imogen, somewhat confused by recent incidents, discovers the decapitated corpse beside her. Because the villainous Cloten had worn Posthumus's clothes, Imogen identifies the body as that of her long absent husband. In frenzied grief and despair, Imogen decides that Pisanio has murdered his master and deceived her. Fainting, she falls on the body.

Lucius, Captains, and a Soothsayer appear. One of the Captains informs Lucius of the expected arrival of reinforcements from Rome under the command of Iachimo. As the Soothsayer is prophesying a Roman victory, Lucius sees the unconscious Fidele (Imogen) lying on the bloody body of Cloten, rouses him, and interrogates him. Fidele tells Lucius that the body is that of Richard de Champ, his master, whom the mountaineers have slain. He says that his own name is Fidele, and Lucius invites the "page" to enter his service. Fidele accepts his offer but requests time to give the body of Cloten suitable burial, a task in which Lucius commands his men to assist.

IV,iii. Britain. Cymbeline's Palace

Cymbeline, sending an attendant to inquire about the health of the Queen, threatens Pisanio with torture unless he divulges the whereabouts of Imogen. Pisanio maintains that he is ignorant of the Princess's movements, and one of the lords vouches for Pisanio's loyalty. Also concerned about Cloten's unexplained absence, Cymbeline shows more distress concerning events in his household than about the Roman legions that have landed in his kingdom. Alone, Pisanio cannot understand why he has received no communication from either Posthumus or Imogen, or any report of Cloten.

IV,iv. Wales. In Front of the Cave of Belarius

Belarius, afraid to return to Cymbeline's court as an outlaw, counsels flight into the mountains. The inborn honor and royal blood of Guiderius and Arviragus lead them to view such action as base, and they persuade Belarius to go with them to enlist with their fellow Britons in their country's defense.

V,i. Britain. The Roman Camp

Having received a bloody cloth from Pisanio as evidence of Imogen's death, Posthumus repents his rashness. Overcome with shame and remorse, he determines to desert the Roman army and join Cymbeline's forces.

V,ii. Britain. A Battlefield between the British and Roman Camps

"Enter Lucius, Iachimo, and the Romane Army at one doore: and the Britaine Army at another: Leonatus Posthumus following like a poore Souldier. They march ouer, and goe out. Then enter againe in Skirmish Iachimo and Posthumus: he vanquisheth and disarmeth Iachimo, and then leaues him." [1]

Iachimo attributes his personal defeat to his defaming and abuse of Imogen, the guilt of the deed weighing heavily upon him. Iachimo leaves, and the battle rages furiously. The British flee. The Romans capture Cymbeline, but Belarius, Guiderius, and Arviragus, assisted by Posthumus, rescue the King and depart. Lucius, Iachimo, and Imogen (as Fidele) appear, and the Roman commander urges Fidele to desert and save himself.

V,iii. Another Part of the Field

Posthumus describes to a British Lord the remarkable prowess and miraculous victory of Belarius, Guiderius, and Arviragus, who saved Cymbeline against overwhelming odds. Posthumus loses patience and satirizes the Lord, who has shown cowardice in battle. Then, in a short soliloquy, Posthumus regrets that he has not found the death he sought and resolves to surrender himself "to the veriest hind" who first appears. When two British Captains and soldiers approach, Posthumus yields himself to them as a Roman. They present him as a captive to Cymbeline, who arrives with his army and several Roman prisoners, among whom is Lucius.

V,iv. Britain. A Prison

Two Jailors leave Posthumus securely confined in irons. Hoping that death may speedily free him from his bondage, Posthumus falls asleep and dreams.

Apparitions, representing Posthumus's deceased father and mother and two brothers, circle Posthumus as they invoke the aid of Jupiter

[1] This is the stage direction in the First Folio.

in song. Jupiter, descending on an eagle in thunder and lightning, throws a thunderbolt, and the ghosts fall to their knees. Assuring the Apparitions that happier days are in store for Posthumus and ordering them to place a tablet on Posthumus's breast and depart, Jupiter ascends. The ghost of Sicilius (father of Posthumus) advises the other spirits that they should perform Jupiter's commands, and they vanish.

Waking, Posthumus reads the cryptic message that promises an auspicious future for him and for Britain. A Jailor reappears, and he and Posthumus mockingly discuss the prisoner's imminent execution. While they are talking, a messenger enters with orders to release Posthumus from his fetters and convey him to the King.

V,v. Britain. Cymbeline's Tent

In the presence of his court, Cymbeline offers a reward to anyone who can find the "poor soldier" who fought so gallantly in the recent battle. Turning to Belarius, Guiderius, and Arviragus, Cymbeline thanks them and knights them for their loyal service. At this point Cornelius appears with several ladies-in-waiting and describes the death of the Queen. With the corroboration of the ladies, the physician relates how the Queen confessed: (1) that she never loved the King but married him for his position; (2) that she arranged for the poisoning of Imogen; and (3) that she planned to murder the King and set Cloten on the throne. Frustrated by the unexplained disappearance of her son, the Queen "despairing died." Admitting that the Queen grossly deceived him, Cymbeline turns to address the Roman captives, who now enter accompanied by Posthumus and Fidele.

Cymbeline tells Lucius that his life and the lives of his fellow prisoners are forfeit and to prepare for death. Accepting this cold reality, Lucius nevertheless asks mercy for Fidele, "a Briton born, . . . so kind, so duteous, diligent," who has done no Briton harm although he served a Roman. Finding something familiar about the page Fidele, Cymbeline grants his life and tells him to ask any boon he wishes. Lucius interposes that, although he does not request Fidele's intercession, he knows that the page will ask Cymbeline's pardon for his master. To Lucius's chagrin, Fidele tells him that his life must shuffle for itself because "There's other work in hand."

While Cymbeline and Fidele converse aside, Belarius and the two kidnaped princes recognize Fidele, and Pisanio identifies the page as his mistress. Having reached an understanding, Cymbeline returns with Fidele and commands Iachimo to step forward and answer the page's questions truthfully. Pointing to the ring on Iachimo's finger, Fidele demands that the Italian tell how he got possession of it. In detail, Iachimo relates the circumstances of the wager and his duplicity in claiming that he had fulfilled the conditions of the bet. Unable to restrain himself further, Posthumus advances, denounces Iachimo, and declares that he himself deserves torture and death for mistrusting his virtuous and faithful wife.

When Fidele interrupts him, Posthumus strikes him for being a "scornful page," and Pisanio shouts that Posthumus has "ne'er killed Imogen till now." Pisanio revives Imogen, who accuses him of attempting to poison her. Cornelius allays the confusion by disclosing how he thwarted the Queen's purpose with the supposedly deadly prescriptions. In the midst of the universal rejoicing and identification of Imogen, Pisanio reveals Cloten's departure in Posthumus's clothes, and Guiderius says that he killed Cloten in Wales, Regretfully, Cymbeline informs Guiderius that he must suffer the death penalty for having killed Cloten, who was a prince as well as a rascal, and orders the guard to bind the youth.

Belarius cautions Cymbeline that Guiderius is a better man than Cloten was and "as well descended" as the King. To quell the mounting rage and indignation of the King, Belarius identifies himself as the banished traitor instead of the supposed Morgan. He proceeds to tell how he kidnaped the princes, married their nurse, Euriphile, and trained the boys for twenty years. For proof Belarius offers to produce the "most curious mantle" which Arviragus wore, and he also mentions a distinguishing birthmark on Guiderius's neck. Rejoicing in the repossession of his three children, Cymbeline postpones a further recital of events until after a general thanksgiving in the temple. As a part of the celebration, Cymbeline grants amnesty to all the Roman prisoners but wishes that the "forlorn soldier" could appear to claim his reward.

Posthumus identifies himself as the much-sought soldier and invites Iachimo to support his statement. Returning the ring and bracelet, Iachimo invites Posthumus to kill him in atonement. Generously Posthumus forgives him and spares his life. He then calls forward the Soothsayer (Philarmonus) to read and interpret the cryptic paper that he found on his breast when he woke in prison (V,iv). As part of the prophecy's fulfillment, Cymbeline proclaims that in victory he will submit to Caesar and the Roman Empire, pay the tribute, and let the Roman and the British flags wave in peace together.

THE WINTER'S TALE [1610–1611]

CHARACTERS

LEONTES, King of Sicilia.

MAMILLIUS, his son, young Prince of Sicilia.

CAMILLO,
ANTIGONUS,
CLEOMENES,
DION, } lords of Sicilia.

POLIXENES, King of Bohemia.

FLORIZEL [*Doricles*], his son, Prince of Bohemia.

ARCHIDAMUS, a lord of Bohemia.

OLD SHEPHERD, reputed father of *Perdita*.

CLOWN, his son.

AUTOLYCUS, a rogue.

A Mariner.

A Jailor.

TIME, as Chorus.

HERMIONE, Queen to *Leontes*.

PERDITA, daughter to *Leontes* and *Hermione*.

PAULINA, wife to *Antigonus*.

EMILIA, a lady attending on the Queen.

MOPSA,
DORCAS, } shepherdesses.

Other Lords, Gentlemen, Ladies, Officers, Servants, Shepherds, and Shepherdesses.

Scene: *Sicilia; Bohemia*

I,i. Sicilia. The Palace of Leontes

Camillo and Archidamus are discussing the lifelong friendship between Leontes and Polixenes, a relationship they believe nothing can mar or alter. Camillo thinks that Leontes will visit Bohemia during the coming summer, and Archidamus praises the character and talents of Prince Mamillius.

I,ii. Sicilia. The Palace of Leontes

Having been away from home for nine months, Polixenes informs Leontes and Hermione that he must end his visit with them the next day. When his appeals that Polixenes prolong his stay are unavailing, Leontes urges Hermione to add her invitation. Speaking eloquently and graciously, Hermione induces Polixenes to remain a week longer. Leontes tells her that the only time she ever spoke to better purpose was when she accepted his proposal of marriage. Delighted with her husband's compliment, Hermione gives her hand to Polixenes to seal his promise to stay. Instantly Leontes yields to a fit of jealousy. While his suspicions of Hermione's infidelity mount, Leontes chats with Mamillius. Hermione and Polixenes note the rising distraction and emotion in Leontes's manner, but he explains it by saying that Mamillius makes him recall his boyhood.

Exhorting Hermione to extend all hospitality to Polixenes, Leontes takes leave of his wife and friend in order to walk with Mamillius. In a moment, wildly jealous thoughts possess him; he sends Mamillius to play and converses with Camillo. Innocently unaware of the King's unreasoning suspicions, Camillo agrees that Polixenes has yielded to Hermione's entreaties when he would not comply with Leontes's. To Camillo's astonishment, Leontes accuses him of betraying trust, of being a coward, or of being stupid in not having reported Hermione's infidelity.

Horrified, Camillo upholds the good reputation of the Queen and advises Leontes to be cured of this "most dangerous" and "diseas'd" opinion." When Camillo persists in denying the allegations against the Queen, Leontes calls him a liar and insists that Polixenes is her illicit partner. The King suggests that Camillo, as cupbearer, poison Polixenes. Camillo admits that he could arrange to do this easily and without arousing suspicion, but he still cannot believe that the Queen is guilty. After Leontes argues that he would not thus sully his own honor without cause and promises not to besmirch the name of Hermione, Camillo apparently consents to perform the King's wishes. Resolved to conceal his true purpose behind a friendly appearance, Leontes leaves. In a short soliloquy, Camillo says that he will forsake Sicilia before he kills an anointed king.

Polixenes, pondering the cooling of his welcome in Sicilia, finds Camillo and asks him why his host's manner has changed. At first Camillo steadfastly refuses to enlighten Polixenes, but under repeated demands he finally tells Polixenes that he is appointed to murder him. Saying that it is safer to "Avoid what's grown than question how 'tis born," Camillo advises Polixenes to leave that very night and volunteers to assist him in his departure. Gratefully,

Polixenes accepts Camillo's offer to enter his service, and the two
men start their preparations to flee.

II,i. Sicilia. The Palace of Leontes

In the presence of Hermione, her ladies and Mamillius playfully
talk about cosmetics and the Queen's advanced pregnancy. Hermione
coaxes Mamillius to tell her a story as Leontes, Antigonus, and
other lords enter.

One of the lords is describing the embarkation of Polixenes and
Camillo, and the King at once construes their flight as proof of their
complicity and guilt. Angrily Leontes orders his attendants to remove
Mamillius from Hermione and says that she may sport herself with
the infant she is about to bear to Polixenes. In blunt and coarse
words, Leontes calls Hermione an adulteress and a traitor. Deaf to
her calm and dignified protestations of innocence, he orders her and
her ladies conveyed to prison under guard. Antigonus and a lord
vigorously defend Hermione's reputation and implore their master to
retract his judgment and action. Insisting that they are fools not
to accept clear and positive evidence, Leontes says that he has
dispatched Cleomenes and Dion to Delphos to secure the opinion
of the oracle of Apollo as additional confirmation. Pending their
return, he has ordered the imprisonment of Hermione to insure security to his own person and to the state.

II,ii. Sicilia. A Prison

Paulina sends an attendant to summon the Jailor, who refuses to
conduct Paulina to the Queen but calls Emilia out. In the presence
of the Jailor, Emilia tells Paulina that Hermione has given birth to
a daughter. Thinking that sight of the child may soften Leontes's
heart, Paulina enlists Emilia's help in persuading Hermione to yield
custody of the infant. Paulina also convinces the Jailor that he may
permit her to release the babe if Hermione agrees to the plan.

II,iii. Sicilia. The Palace of Leontes

Tortured by his jealous thoughts and knowing that Polixenes is
beyond reach, Leontes ponders how he can punish Hermione. He
inquires concerning the health of Mamillius, who has taken ill
(Leontes supposes) because of his mother's dishonor and disgrace.
As schemes of revenge pass through Leontes's mind, Paulina brings
in the newborn Princess. Defying orders for her removal, Paulina lays
the baby in front of Leontes and tells him that Hermione commends

it to his blessing. Denouncing Paulina as a witch and calling the child a bastard, Leontes commands Antigonus to return the infant to Paulina. Boldly forbidding her husband to touch the babe and in face of the King's threats, Paulina proclaims the legitimacy of the child and leaves.

In a rage, Leontes orders Antigonus to be personally responsible for the instant burning of the infant and charges him with being Hermione's and Paulina's accomplice. Antigonus and the other lords assert his innocence, but Leontes calls them all liars. In the face of their insistent pleading, Leontes relents and tells Antigonus that he may save the "brat's life" if he swears to take the child to a foreign country and abandon it in "some remote and desert place." Reluctantly, Antigonus vows to comply with the order and carries the infant out.

A servant reports the miraculously speedy return of Cleomenes and Dion from Delphos, and Leontes proclaims the public arraignment and trial of Hermione.

III,i. Sicilia. A Road

Cleomenes and Dion, hastening toward the capital, recall the rituals and features of Delphos, congratulate themselves on their successful journey, and hope that the sealed opinion of the oracle will prove gracious and propitious to the Queen.

III,ii. Sicilia. A Court of Justice

Leontes expresses confidence that the ensuing trial of Hermione will clear him of any accusation of tyranny. An officer orders Hermione to stand before the court. She enters with Paulina and other ladies, and the officer reads the indictment charging her with adultery with Polixenes, with conspiracy with Camillo to murder Leontes, and with aiding both men to flee by night.

In opening her defense, Hermione recalls her own royal ancestry, her motherhood of Mamillius, and her impeccable conduct prior to the visit of Polixenes. Continuing, she admits that she loved Polixenes chastely as an intimate friend of Leontes and as her husband had himself commanded and required of her. Furthermore, she characterizes Camillo as an honest man and denies any knowledge of why he left Sicilia.

Obstinately, Leontes declares Hermione guilty of adultery and falsehood, and says that she must expect the death penalty. Unfrightened by his threats, Hermione replies that after the loss of her husband's favor, the removal of Mamillius, the murder of her newborn infant, and her public indictment and trial, she has no desire to live. Life means nothing to her, honor everything. Therefore she will appeal to the Delphian oracle.

Pronouncing her request "altogether just," Leontes commands his officers to usher in Cleomenes and Dion. After both men have sworn that they visited Delphos, secured the oracle from Apollo's priest, and have neither broken the seal nor read the contents, an officer opens the document and reads it. In substance the oracle declares the innocence of Hermione, Polixenes, and Camillo, and the legitimacy of the infant. It also calls Leontes "a jealous tyrant" and says, "the King shall live without an heir, if that which is lost be not found." In spite of Hermione's relief and the pleasure of his lords, Leontes asserts, "There is no truth at all i' th' oracle:/The sessions shall proceed: this is mere falsehood."

At this instant, a servant appears with news that Mamillius, concerned about his mother's fate, has died. Leontes says that an angry Apollo and the heavens are punishing his injustice, and Hermione swoons. Finally realizing that he has yielded too far to his suspicions, Leontes orders Paulina and other attendants to take Hermione out and care for her. To those remaining in court, Leontes proclaims the integrity of all whom he has accused and confesses his own jealous villainy.

Paulina returns and shames Leontes by recalling his betrayal of Polixenes, his defamation of Camillo, and his harsh removal of the infant daughter. These acts, she says, branded Leontes as a jealous, tyrannical, foolish ingrate. No one can charge him with direct responsibility for the death of Mamillius, but he must answer for a final catastrophe—the death of Hermione. Contrite and repentant, Leontes admits that he deserves all of Paulina's harsh words. A lord admonishes Paulina that she has been too bold in her speech, and the faithful woman says that love for Hermione made her rash. She invites Leontes to punish her. The King commends her for having spoken truth and directs her to arrange the burial of Hermione and Mamillius in the same tomb, which he will visit once every day as long as he lives.

III,iii. Bohemia. The Seacoast

Antigonus, carrying the infant, appears with a Mariner. A storm is threatening. Antigonus tells the Mariner to return aboard ship and that he will soon join him. Glad to comply, the Mariner warns Antigonus of wild animals and departs. Talking to the babe, Antigonus relates a vision in which Hermione directed him to abandon the child in Bohemia and to name it Perdita. The creature in the dream also advised him that he would never again see Paulina. Ordinarily skeptical of visions, Antigonus nevertheless decides to yield to what he regards as superstition. Depositing a written identification and a package beside the infant, Antigonus starts back to the ship, a bear pursuing him.

A Shepherd, searching for two lost sheep, discovers the abandoned babe. While he speculates on the sex and origin of the child, his son, the Clown, joins him. Excitedly, the Clown describes the foundering of the ship in the storm and the bear's devouring of Antigonus. Together the Shepherd and the Clown inspect the infant and the treasure Antigonus left with her. Forsaking their sheep, they arrange for the Shepherd to take the child and the gold home while the Clown buries what the bear has left of Antigonus.

IV,i

Time, as Chorus, recounts the passing of sixteen years. In Sicilia, Leontes secludes himself in grief. In Bohemia, Florizel is the princely son of Polixenes, and Perdita passes for the Shepherd's daughter.

IV,ii. Bohemia. The Palace of Polixenes

Camillo seeks Polixenes's permission to return to Sicilia. Polixenes protests that Camillo has made himself indispensable and inquires the whereabouts of Florizel, who has frequently absented himself from court and has been neglecting his "princely exercises." Polixenes has heard that Florizel often visits the home of a prosperous shepherd, and Camillo adds that the man has a daughter of unusual charm. Camillo agrees to postpone his departure in order that he and Polixenes may disguise themselves and interview the shepherd and determine the cause of Florizel's interest.

IV,iii. Bohemia. A Road near the Shepherd's Cottage

Autolycus, a tinker and roguish thief who has been in Florizel's service but is out of employment, appears singing. He sees the Clown approaching and plans to deceive him. While the Clown audibly calculates the price of wool and enumerates the items Perdita has ordered for the sheepshearing feast, Autolycus grovels on the ground and cries for help. Charitably, the Clown lends assistance, and Autolycus picks his pocket. When the Clown offers to give Autolycus a little money, the rascal quickly declines to accept it lest his victim detect the crime. Claiming to have been robbed and abused, Autolycus describes and names himself as the bandit. The Clown resumes his way to market, and Autolycus gloats over his thievery.

IV,iv. Bohemia. In Front of the Shepherd's Cottage

Florizel and Perdita are talking about their special costumes for the feast. Florizel is thankful for the chance which brought them together, but Perdita is worried about the difference in their social rank. She is also concerned lest some coincidence lead Polixenes to discover them. She speculates that the King will forbid their love match, but Florizel vows that he will disown his father before he forsakes their sworn nuptial.

Guests are arriving, and at the behest of Florizel and the Shepherd, Perdita graciously welcomes Polixenes and Camillo, both of whom are disguised. Perdita gaily distributes flowers to her guests. She wishes that she had an abundance of special posies with which to make garlands for Florizel, whom she and her companions call Doricles. The merriment increases until Perdita, Florizel, Mopsa, Dorcas, the Clown, and others begin to dance.

Polixenes and Camillo have observed the romantic attachment between Florizel and Perdita, and during the dance, Polixenes questions the Shepherd about his "daughter" and Florizel. Praising the talents of Perdita, the Shepherd says that each loves the other and that if they wed she will bring Doricles more than he dreams of.

A servant announces the arrival of peddler with a variety of wares and an inexhaustible repertory of tunes and ballads. Autolycus enters with a song proclaiming his merchandise. Mopsa and Dorcas beg the Clown to purchase them numerous trinkets and favors, and they sing through one of the ballads. Autolycus leaves, and rustics render "a Dance of twelve Satyrs."

Deciding that matters have gone far enough, Polixenes asks Florizel why he has not purchased some of the peddler's wares for Perdita. Florizel replies that she values his heart more than such trifles and that he would forsake all titles and possessions for her love. Polixenes and Camillo pretend to approve his avowal. After Perdita confesses a similar love for Florizel, the Shepherd sanctions the betrothal and calls Polixenes and Camillo to witness that he will give Perdita a wedding portion equal to the bridegroom's.

Here Polixenes interrupts to ask Florizel if he has a father and if his father should not be a party to these arrangements. Although

Polixenes and the Shepherd beg him to inform his parent, Florizel insists that this is impossible. Revealing his true identity, Polixenes forbids the wedding, denounces Florizel as base and unworthy, and threatens to execute the Shepherd for treason. A moment later Polixenes revokes the sentence of death on the Shepherd, but vows to disinherit Florizel and put Perdita to the torture if they meet again. He departs, and Perdita, whose worst fears have materialized, begs Florizel to follow his father.

Still believing that he will die, the Shepherd rebukes Florizel and Perdita for deceiving him and causing his adversity. Florizel, undaunted, renews his determination to marry Perdita. Camillo warns him against trying to approach Polixenes while the King is still enraged, and Florizel recognizes the faithful counselor. Renouncing his title to the throne of Bohemia, Florizel begs Camillo to calm the King's passion while he and Perdita make their escape on a ship he has waiting nearby. Seeing an opportunity whereby he may arrange his own eventual return to his native land, Camillo advises Florizel to marry Perdita, sail for Sicilia, and seek protection and shelter with Leontes. Camillo will provide Florizel with information and documents enabling him to present himself as a personal envoy from his father. In the meantime, Camillo will endeavor to placate Polixenes. In addition, he will supply Florizel and Perdita with royal appointments and effects from his own fortune in Sicilia. While they chat to one side, Autolycus returns.

In a soliloquy, the rogue describes how he has disposed of all his wares and how he might easily have stolen everybody's purse had not the Shepherd's hubbub dispersed the feasters. Seeing the rags Autolycus is wearing, Camillo bribes him to exchange clothes with Florizel. Perdita will disguise herself by rearranging her apparel and donning Florizel's hat. Hastily Camillo conducts them to the ship. In an aside, he discloses that he will inform Polixenes of their flight and induce him to pursue them to Sicilia.

Autolycus, shrewdly aware of what has taken place, wonders if he should embrace honesty and inform Polixenes but decides that he can prove the greater knave by concealing what he knows. Seeing the Shepherd and the Clown approaching with a parcel, Autolycus steps aside to eavesdrop on them. They have decided to go to Polixenes and tell their entire story in hope of clearing themselves. Autolycus removes the false beard he has been wearing, addresses the Shepherd and his son, convinces them that he is a courtier, and asks them the contents of the package. Pretending not to know who the Shepherd is, Autolycus tells him that the King has sailed and that the Shepherd and his son are certain to suffer agonizing punishments and death. Autolycus then offers to act as their advocate in whatever suit they may wish to present to Polixenes. Thoroughly impressed with Autolycus and badly frightened, the Shepherd and the Clown promise to reward him liberally if he will represent them before the King. Once again the rogue foresees the chance of double profit if he can sell his information to Polixenes.

V,i. Sicilia. The Palace of Leontes

Cleomenes and Dion are vigorously advising Leontes to cease his penance and remarry in order that the throne may have a successor. Paulina bluntly tells Leontes that the world does not hold a woman equal to the wife he killed. Furthermore, she reminds them that the oracle prophesied that the King would not have an heir "Till his lost child be found." Leontes admits the soundness of Paulina's reasoning and says that he does not wish to marry again lest Hermione's ghost haunt him and her successor. At Paulina's insistence, Leontes swears that he will remarry only if she chooses the bride and bids him wed her. "That," Paulina says, "Shall be when your first queen's again in breath;/Never till then."

A servant announces the arrival of Prince Florizel and his Princess. Surprised at the unceremonious circumstances of their visit, Leontes nevertheless directs Cleomenes to escort the guests before him. Florizel, whose similarity to his father astonishes Leontes, tells his host that he has come to Sicilia by his father's command, that his bride is from Libya, and that he has sent most of his attendants on to Bohemia to report his marriage and his safe arrival.

No sooner has Leontes warmly welcomed the young couple than a lord enters with a request from Polixenes, who has just reached the city, to arrest Florizel, who is eloping with a shepherd's daughter. The lord adds the information that Polixenes has, on the way, met Perdita's father and brother (the Old Shepherd and the Clown). Florizel jumps to the conclusion that Camillo has betrayed him, and the lord describes how Camillo and Polixenes are questioning and threatening the two rustics. Perdita exclaims that the heavens are opposed to her wedding with Florizel, and Florizel admits to Leontes that they have not yet solemnized their marriage. Reaffirming his constant love for Perdita, Florizel beseeches Leontes to intercede with Polixenes on his behalf. Commenting that he would gladly have Perdita for his own bride, Leontes agrees to do what he can.

V,ii. Sicilia. In Front of the Palace of Leontes

Three gentlemen and Autolycus discuss the universal joy attending the identification of Perdita as the long-lost princess and the disclosure of her rescue and betrothal to Florizel. Less joyous was Leontes's confession to Perdita of the manner and cause of Hermione's death. All have gone to the house where Paulina has superintended the creation of a lifelike statue of Hermione by "that rare Italian master, Julio Romano." The gentlemen depart for Paulina's house, and the Shepherd and the Clown approach, congratulating themselves on their advancement in society. Autolycus asks them to give him a good reference to the King. After the rogue promises that he will reform, they decide that their new status as gentlemen demands generosity and promise to sponsor him.

V,iii. Sicilia. A Chapel in Paulina's House

Leontes has inspected many rare pieces in Paulina's art collection, but he is impatient to see the statue of Hermione. Explaining that she has kept it apart from the others because of its surpassing excellence, Paulina draws a curtain and reveals Hermione standing like a statue.

Leontes marvels at the likelike posture of the statue but observes that the real Hermione "was not so much wrinkled" or as aged as the sculpture. Paulina says that this merely testifies to the expertness of the artist, who could thus portray the Queen as she would have become after sixteen years. Overcome with emotion, Leontes addresses the statue with pathetic contrition, and Perdita kneels and attempts to kiss its hand. Camillo and Polixenes try to console Leontes. Paulina declares that she did not anticipate such a violent reaction by Leontes and starts to drop the curtain, but he begs her to leave the figure exposed. Cleverly Paulina leads Leontes to ascribe movement, breath, and warmth to the statue. Finally Paulina tells him that he must leave the chapel or be prepared for her to make the statue move, descend, and take him by the hand. Emphasizing that she is not employing black magic, Paulina orders music and commands the statue to step from the pedestal. To everyone's amazement, Hermione walks down and embraces Leontes. Paulina commends all to their happiness and says that she will isolate herself to mourn for Antigonus.

Reconciled to Hermione and Polixenes, Leontes seals the match between Florizel and Perdita and directs Camillo to marry Paulina.

THE TEMPEST [1611–1612]

CHARACTERS

ALONSO, King of Naples.

SEBASTIAN, his brother.

PROSPERO, the Duke of Milan.

ANTONIO, his brother, the usurping Duke of Milan.

FERDINAND, son to the King of Naples.

GONZALO, an honest old counsellor.

ADRIAN,
FRANCISCO, } lords.

CALIBAN, a savage and deformed slave.

TRINCULO, a jester.

STEPHANO, a drunken butler.

Master of a ship.

Boatswain.

Mariners.

MIRANDA, daughter to *Prospero.*

ARIEL, an airy spirit.

IRIS,
CERES,
JUNO, } spirits.
Nymphs,
Reapers,

Other Spirits attending on *Prospero.*

Scene: *A Ship at Sea; an Uninhabited Island*

I,i. A Ship at Sea. A Tempestuous Noise of Thunder and Lightning

On the Shipmaster's command the Boatswain exhorts the Mariners to bestir themselves. Alonso and his party come on deck to survey the storm, but the Boatswain tells them that they are in the way and orders them to their cabins. Gonzalo remonstrates, but they withdraw as the Boatswain directs the seamen to lower the topmast. In a moment, Sebastian, Antonio, and Gonzalo reappear while the Boatswain drives his crew to renewed efforts to save the ship. Just as the passengers decide to assist the crew, cries of "We split, we split," come from within, and all prepare to "sink wi' th' King."

I,ii. The Island. In Front of Prospero's Cell

Miranda, who has witnessed the breaking up of the ship and the suffering of those aboard it, pleads with her father to allay the storm. Prospero assures her that "There's no harm done" and that he has contrived everything in care of her. Reminding her that she knows nothing of his origin or her own, he tells her to remove his "magic garment" from him, to sit down, and to listen to his account of the past. Again he states that no one aboard the ship has incurred injury.

Although Miranda was only three years old when she came to the island, she has a vague recollection of four or five women who waited on her before. Prospero recalls that twelve years have elapsed since he, absorbed in "the liberal arts" and "rapt in secret studies," delegated the power of government to his brother Antonio. Seizing this opportunity, Antonio entered into league with the King of Naples, who banished Prospero and conferred the dukedom on Antonio. Afraid to murder Prospero and Miranda because of the people's love for the rightful duke, Alonso and Antonio set the fugitives adrift at sea on "A rotten carcass of a butt" without tackle, sail, or mast.

Fortunately, Gonzalo, a noble Neapolitan, "Out of his charity" provided the castaways with food, fresh water, clothing, necessaries, and a few books that Prospero prized above his dukedom. Strengthened with the smiles of his young daughter, Prospero succeeded in reaching the island, where he has devoted most of his time to instructing Miranda. Aware that his enemies were approaching the island by ship, Prospero raised the storm in order to restore himself to power.

Seeing that Miranda has fallen asleep, Prospero summons Ariel, who reports how he has executed his master's commands. The ship rides safely in harbor; the passengers are scattered in groups about the island, Ferdinand by himself; the Mariners are soundly sleeping below deck; the remainder of the convoy has returned to Naples with word of Alonso's drowning.

Prospero commends Ariel but says that they have more toil ahead of them. Ariel protests that Prospero has promised him his freedom for faithful service, but Prospero says that the time has not yet come. He recalls how the "damn'd witch Sycorax," banished from Algiers "For mischiefs manifold, and sorceries terrible," brought Ariel to the island and punished him for disobedience by confining him "Into a cloven pine." For twelve years Ariel remained imprisoned, during which time Sycorax died and left her son Caliban as the only other inhabitant of the island. Reminding Ariel that he escaped only through Prospero's magic power, Prospero threatens to fasten him in an oak, unless he submits to orders. Upon Ariel's renewal of loyalty, Prospero promises to discharge him after two days and commands him to change himself into a nymph of the sea and depart.

Miranda wakens, and Prospero takes her to visit Caliban, "a villain" she does not "love to look on." Ariel returns in the form of a water nymph, receives instructions, and leaves. Grumbling that he has inherited title to the island from his mother and that Prospero is a usurper, Caliban appears in response to Prospero's calls. The monster repents of having shown Prospero "all the qualities o' th' isle" and resents the harsh treatment he has received, but Prospero reminds Caliban of his attempted violation of Miranda. Caliban's only regret is that he failed to people the "isle with Calibans." Describing the slave as a brutish, stupid thing, Prospero sends him to fetch fuel. Knowing that Prospero's power is greater than that of Setebos, the god of Sycorax, Caliban sets about his chores.

Ferdinand appears, trying to find the source of the music and song supplied by the invisible Ariel. Prospero asks Miranda to identify Ferdinand, and the girl replies that "it" must be a spirit or a "thing divine." Ferdinand addresses Miranda and is amazed when she answers in his own language. Prospero discerns their mutual infatuation and praises Ariel for skillfully carrying out his orders.

Charmed with Miranda, Ferdinand promises to make her Queen of Naples, since he now assumes himself to have succeeded his father to the throne. Prospero intervenes, however, to charge Ferdinand with spying and attempting to seize the island. Resisting arrest, Ferdinand draws his sword, but Prospero renders him unable to move. Miranda intercedes for Ferdinand. Admonishing his daughter that the youth is far less handsome than she supposes him to be, Prospero gives further instructions to Ariel and escorts the young couple away.

II,i. Another Part of the Island

Antonio, Alonso, and their attending lords attempt to silence Gonzalo, who persists in finding favorable features in their present condition on the island. Alonso expresses concern for the loss of Ferdinand, although Francisco saw him swimming strongly and thinks that he may have gained the shore. Sebastian tartly blames Alonso's obstinacy for the catastrophe, since the King insisted on embarking on the voyage against the advice of his counselors. Gonzalo remarks that Sebastian rubs the sore when he should "bring the plaster." Attempting to cheer the others, Gonzalo speculates on the society he would institute on the island if he had power to do so, but they cynically mock his idealism. Ariel, invisible to the party, enters "playing solemn music," and all except Alonso, Sebastian, and Antonio fall asleep. In a moment Alonso also sleeps.

Carefully feeling each other out, Sebastian and Antonio convince themselves that Ferdinand has drowned and that his sister Claribel (recently married to the King of Tunis) is too far from Naples to claim succession to its throne. They decide that Antonio will slay Alonso and that Sebastian will kill Gonzalo at the same time. Thus Sebastian will become King of Naples, and Antonio will be free from paying tribute. They draw their weapons, but before they can strike, Ariel sings in Gonzalo's ear and wakens him. Gonzalo shakes Alonso, and he asks Sebastian and Antonio why they are standing with naked swords. The two conspirators excuse themselves by claiming to have heard the noise of wild beasts. Gonzalo, who "heard a humming," thinks that they should remain on guard or leave the place. Ariel goes to report the episode to Prospero.

II,ii. Another Part of the Island

Caliban, struggling under a load of wood to the accompaniment of thunder, sees Trinculo and thinks that he is a spirit Prospero has sent to torment him for "bringing wood in slowly." Caliban lies down in the hope that Trinculo will not notice him. Trinculo, searching for shelter from the approaching storm, sees Caliban. In spite of Caliban's "very ancient and fish-like smell" Trinculo decides that "this is no fish, but an islander, that hath lately suffered by a thunderbolt" and creeps beneath Caliban's cloak.

Stephano, drinking from a bottle and singing a bawdy chantey, hears Caliban's cries of torment and discovers "some monster of the isle, with four legs." Thinking that he has found some remarkable creature that he can tame and later exhibit in Naples, Stephano offers Caliban a couple of drinks from his bottle. Recognizing the butler's voice, Trinculo addresses Stephano, who pulls forth the jester from Caliban's garment. Stephano gives Trinculo a drink and assures him that he has salvaged the whole butt from the seashore. In the meantime Caliban has decided that Stephano is "a brave god and bears celestial liquor" and swears to be his true subject. The butler identifies himself as "the Man i' th' Moon" and gives Caliban another drink. While Trinculo laughs at the idea of a monster's making a wonder of a poor drunkard, Caliban kneels and promises to show Stephano all the resources of the island and to serve as his menial. Believing themselves masters of the island, Stephano and Trinculo follow Caliban, who goes ahead, singing "drunkenly."

III,i. In Front of Prospero's Cell

Ferdinand, carrying a log, reflects upon Prospero's harshness as a taskmaster but finds compensation in Miranda's sympathetic concern. Miranda joins him, urges him to rest while Prospero "Is hard at study," and offers to carry the logs for him. A comment from Prospero, who remains apart from the couple, indicates his awareness that Miranda has become infatuated with Ferdinand. Ferdinand declares that, although he has admired many a lady, Miranda excels all others in perfection and is created "Of every creature's best." Miranda admits that Prospero and Ferdinand are the only men she has ever seen but says that she would not wish any companion in the world but Ferdinand. Happily they pledge their troth to each other and depart. Prospero, who has been anticipating their engagement, voices his approval in a brief soliloquy.

III,ii. Another Part of the Island

Deep in their cups, Stephano, Trinculo, and Caliban are talking about their situation. Trinculo jests at Caliban's expense until Stephano orders him to keep a good tongue in his head. Ariel, who is invisible, hovers near them while Caliban relates Prospero's seizure of the island and suggests that Stephano can seize Prospero's books, kill the "sorcerer," and possess Miranda. Intermittently, Ariel interrupts Caliban by saying, "Thou liest." Stephano and the monster believe that Trinculo is the speaker and threaten him unless he remains quiet and stands farther away. Finally Stephano beats Trinculo but apologizes after the Clown agrees to join the conspiracy. The three rogues sing to celebrate their plot, but again Ariel, who plans to reveal the scheme to Prospero, bedevils them with mysterious noises. Caliban assures his new companions that the island is full of harmless sounds, and they follow the elusive music on their way to slay Prospero.

III,iii. Another Part of the Island

Weary from their fruitless search for Ferdinand, Gonzalo, Alonso, and their companions sit down to rest. Sebastian and Antonio privately agree to make another attempt on the lives of the King and his counselor as soon as they are asleep. Prospero, invisible to the shipwrecked party and accompanied by "solemn and strange music," appears above them and evokes "several strange shapes" that bring in a banquet, dance about it, invite the King and his courtiers to eat, and depart. Greatly amazed, the King and his companions discuss the miracle they have witnessed. Gonzalo assures Alonso that they need not fear to partake of the food. Just as they start to eat, Ariel appears in the shape of a harpy with thunder and lightning, "claps his wings upon the table," and causes the banquet to vanish.

Calling Alonso, Antonio, and Sebastian "three men of sin," Ariel tells them that destiny has caused the sea to belch them up on the island and that they are "most unfit to live." When they draw their swords, Ariel taunts them with their helplessness. He reminds them of their villainous treatment of Prospero and Miranda and tells Alonso that the powers have, in retribution, bereft him of his son. Ariel "vanishes in thunder," and to soft music the Shapes appear again, dance, and mockingly remove the table.

Praising Ariel for his efficiency, Prospero declares that his enemies "are all knit up/In their distractions," and leaves to visit Ferdinand and his beloved Miranda. Gonzalo asks Alonso why he stands "In this strange stare." Alonso interprets the incident as an indictment of his crime and as evidence that Ferdinand has drowned. Sebastian and Antonio determine to attack the supernatural powers. Gonzalo, correctly discerning that guilt is beginning to gnaw at the three men's consciences, urges Adrian and Francisco to follow "And hinder them from what this ecstasy/May provoke them to."

IV,i. In Front of Prospero's Cell

In the presence of Miranda, Prospero tells Ferdinand that his onerous chores have been trials of his love only. He gives his daughter to Ferdinand but sternly warns him that he must not consummate the marriage before "All sanctimonious ceremonies may/With full and holy rite be minist'red." Ferdinand affirms the purity of his love for Miranda, and Prospero tells the two to talk together while he gives additional instructions to Ariel. Wishing to demonstrate his magical power to "this young couple," Prospero orders Ariel to bring his "meaner fellows" before the cell immediately.

Cautioning Ferdinand and Miranda to watch but not to speak, Prospero stages an elaborate masque. Iris appears and summons

Ceres to endow "this grass-plot" with the abundance of harvest in order to entertain Juno, who will soon arrive. Ceres acknowledges Iris's request and learns that Juno has ordained a celebration of the marriage contract between Ferdinand and Miranda. Iris also describes how Ferdinand's vow of premarital chastity has forestalled and thwarted Venus and Cupid, who thought "to have done/Some wanton charm upon this man and maid." Juno now joins the other goddesses and with Ceres sings a blessing on the betrothed couple. Ferdinand, enchanted with this "most majestic vision," says that he would like to live on the island forever, but Prospero silences him as Juno commands the Nymphs and Reapers to dance in honor of the wedding contract. "Towards the end" of the dance Prospero remembers the "foul conspiracy" of Caliban and his accomplices, and after complimenting the Spirits he orders them to depart.

Ferdinand and Miranda note the change that has come over Prospero, who is obviously acting under violent anger. Prospero states that their revels are ended and that the spirits and illusory structures will dissolve like the "insubstantial pageant" they have witnessed. People "are such stuff/As dreams are made on," and man's "little life/Is rounded with a sleep." He is tired and troubled. He sends Ferdinand and Miranda into his cell while he walks to still his "beating mind."

Ariel approaches, and Prospero tells him that they must prepare to meet Caliban. He sends the spirit to fetch "glistering apparel," which he brings back and hangs on a lime tree. Prospero and Ariel remain invisible as Caliban, Stephano, and Trinculo appear, "all wet." The conspirators, who have been drinking heavily, near the entrance of Prospero's cell when Stephano and Trinculo start quarreling over the glistening gown that Ariel has hung on the tree. In vain, Caliban pleads with his companions to dispatch Prospero first and then determine the disposal of the clothes. To the sound of hunting, Prospero and Ariel set "divers Spirits in shape of Dogs and Hounds" on the three rogues and drive them away. Prospero, all his enemies now lying at his mercy, says that his labors will shortly end and Ariel will have his freedom.

V,i. In Front of the Cell of Prospero

Prospero, dressed in "his magic robes," receives Ariel's report. Alonso, Antonio, and Sebastian are "all three distracted" and confined by Prospero's occult power in a grove where their companions mourn over them. The "good old" Gonzalo's grief is especially moving, and

Ariel believes that Prospero would pity his enemies if he beheld them.

Unwilling to concede that Ariel, a spirit, should manifest a greater kindness than he feels as a human, Prospero says, "The rarer action is/In virtue than in vengeance." Since the usurpers are now penitent, Prospero commands Ariel to release them so that he may remove his charms and restore their senses. While Ariel goes on his errand, Prospero renounces his "potent art," abjures his "rough magic," and resolves to break his staff and drown his book.

Ariel escorts Alonso and his attending lords into the magic circle Prospero has made, and they stand charmed in front of Prospero. Concealing his true identity, Prospero praises Gonzalo's virtues and loyalty, denounces Alonso's former cruelty and Antonio's usurpation, and reveals Antonio's and Sebastian's plot on Alonso's life. After forgiving his enemies, Prospero orders Ariel to fetch the hat and rapier he wore as Duke of Milan. Quickly Ariel returns, and Prospero sends him to conduct the Mariners to his cell.

Amazed by the unexpected appearance of the rightful Duke, Gonzalo wishes that some heavenly power would guide him and his companions out of "this fearful country." Presenting himself as the "wronged Duke of Milan," Prospero embraces Alonso and welcomes him to the island. Immediately Alonso restores Prospero's title and asks his pardon. Prospero then embraces Gonzalo, whose "honour cannot/Be measur'd or confin'd." Sebastian, in an aside, attributes Prospero's power to the devil; Antonio is speechless; but Prospero forgives these wicked traitors because he knows they are powerless to prevent his return to his dukedom.

Alonso wants to hear the story of Prospero's preservation on the shore where Ferdinand has perished. Prospero sympathizes with Alonso and says that he has suffered "the like loss" of his daughter. Spontaneously Alonso wishes that "they were living both in Naples./ The King and Queen there!" Informing Alonso that he lost his daughter in the recent storm, Prospero invites the King to look inside his cell where he will see a wonder that will content him. Alonso observes Ferdinand and Miranda playing chess. Sebastian exclaims, "A most high miracle!" and Ferdinand kneels before his father. Miranda, astonished at the number of human beings, says,

> O wonder!
> How many goodly creatures are there here!
> How beauteous mankind is! O brave new world
> That has such people in't!

Ferdinand introduces Miranda to his father, who wholeheartedly approves Gonzalo's thought that the gods have dropped "a blessed crown" on the young couple.

Amid the rejoicing, Ariel brings in the Master of the ship and the Boatswain, who declares that the ship is seaworthy and ready to sail. Alonso listens to the Boatswain's confused recital of the crew's experiences, and Prospero, praising Ariel for his industry, commands the Sprite to release the spell over Caliban and his fellows.

In a moment, Ariel drives in Caliban, Stephano, and Trinculo with their stolen apparel. Prospero presents the trio to the assembled lords, who are making unflattering comments about Caliban. Prospero orders Caliban to take his companions to the cell in hope of receiving pardon, and the monster calls himself "a thrice-double ass" for taking the drunken Stephano for a god and for worshiping Trinculo. Prospero invites Alonso and his train to spend the night on the island while he relates the story of his life for their entertainment. In the morning they will sail for Naples, where Prospero hopes to witness the marriage of Ferdinand and Miranda, after which he will retire to Milan and meditate on death. Charging Ariel to assume responsibility for "calm seas, auspicious gales," Prospero frees his "airy spirit."

Epilogue

Prospero admonishes members of the audience to remember the power of prayer and to show mercy as they would wish to receive it.

CHRONOLOGY OF SHAKESPEARE'S PLAYS

Differences of opinion exist concerning the dates when Shakespeare wrote his plays. A working order is, nevertheless, helpful, and the following sequence, with a slight overlapping of periods, represents a consensus of leading editors and scholars.

Dates	Comedies	Histories	Tragedies
1589–1595	*Comedy of Errors* *Taming of the Shrew* *Two Gentlemen of Verona* *Love's Labour's Lost*	*1 Henry VI* *2 Henry VI* *3 Henry VI* *Richard III*	*Titus Andronicus*
1594–1602	*Midsummer Night's Dream* *Merchant of Venice* *Much Ado about Nothing* *Merry Wives of Windsor* *As You Like It* *Twelfth Night*	*Richard II* *King John* *1 Henry IV* *2 Henry IV* *Henry V*	*Romeo and Juliet* *Julius Caesar*
1600–1609	*Troilus and Cressida* *All's Well That Ends Well* *Measure for Measure* *Pericles*		*Hamlet* *Othello* *King Lear* *Macbeth* *Timon of Athens* *Antony and Cleopatra* *Coriolanus*
1609–1613	*Cymbeline* *Winter's Tale* *Tempest*	*Henry VIII*	

INDEX TO CHARACTERS IN SHAKESPEARE'S COMEDIES

Key to abbreviations:

Abbess. *See* Aemilia
Abhorson, *Meas.*
Achilles, *Troi.*
Adam, *A.Y.L.I.*
[Adam], *Shrew*
Adrian, *Temp.*
Adriana, *Errors*
Aegeon, *Errors*
Aemilia, *Errors*
Aeneas, *Troi.*
Agamemnon, *Troi.*
Aguecheek. *See* Andrew Aguecheek
Ajax, *Troi.*
Alexander, *Troi.*
Aliena. *See* Celia
Alonso, *Temp.*

Amiens, *A.Y.L.I.*
Andrew Aguecheek, Sir, *Twel.*
Andromache, *Troi.*
Angelo, *Errors*
Angelo, *Meas.*
Anne Page. *See* Page, Anne
Antenor, *Troi.*
Anthony Dull. *See* Dull
Antigonus, *Wint.*
Antiochus, *Per.*
Antiochus, Daughter of, *Per.*
Antipholus of Ephesus, *Errors*
Antipholus of Syracuse, *Errors*
Antonio, *Merch.*
Antonio, *Much*
Antonio, *Temp.*